Seeing through a Donor's Eyes

How to Make a Persuasive Case for Everything
from Your Annual Drive to Your Planned Giving Program
to Your Capital Campaign

Of Related Interest

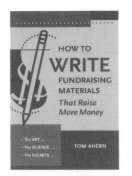

How to Write Fundraising Materials that Raise More Money
The Art ... The Science ... The Secrets

By Tom Ahern, Emerson & Church, Publishers.
ISBN 978-1-889102-31-3, 187 pp., $24.95.

Writing to raise money takes more than a few choice words.

Highly profitable communications use a wide array of "trade secrets" to boost response. Things like emotional triggers, a working knowledge of reader psychology, the discovery of eye motion studies, and donor research – all help writing pros reap big rewards from their appeal letters, newsletters, websites, case statements, and more.

Now these trade secrets are yours, collected in one easy-to-understand volume. Tom Ahern reveals all: how top fundraising writers inspire their prospects to make that first gift – and how they keep existing donors loyal and generous.

The Fundraiser's Guide to Irresistible Communications

By Jeff Brooks, Emerson & Church, Publishers.
ISBN 978-1-889102-03-0, 123 pp., $24.95.

Here it is: a book that reveals what really works in fundraising. Not academic theory or wishful thinking, but ways of communicating that are proven to motivate donors to give generously, wholeheartedly, and repeatedly.

Drawing from decades of in-the-trenches experience, Jeff Brooks, one of America's top fundraising writers, takes you on a step-by-step tour of the unique strategies, writing style, and design techniques of irresistible fundraising messages.

This easy-to-read and entertaining book will help you skip years of learning curve and start writing, designing, and thinking like a seasoned fundraising pro on the very next project you undertake.

Whether you're new to fundraising or a battle-scarred veteran, this book will be your go-to resource and will boost your confidence, your careers, and your revenue.

Emerson & Church, Publishers
www.emersonandchurch.com

Seeing through a Donor's Eyes

How to Make a Persuasive Case for Everything
from Your Annual Drive to Your Planned Giving Program
to Your Capital Campaign

Tom Ahern

Emerson
& Church
PUBLISHERS

www.emersonandchurch.com

First printed February 2009

10 9 8 7 6 5

Printed in the United States of America

This text is printed on acid-free paper.

Copies of this book are available from the publisher at discount when purchased in quantity for boards of directors or staff.

Emerson & Church, Publishers
15 Brooks Street • Medfield, MA 02052
Tel. 508-359-0019 • Fax 508-359-2703
www.emersonandchurch.com

Library of Congress Cataloging-in-Publication Data

Ahern, Tom.
  Seeing through a donor's eyes : how to make a persuasive case for everything from your annual drive to your planned giving program to your capital campaign / by Tom Ahern.
     p. cm.
  ISBN 1-889102-34-2 (pbk. : alk. paper)
  1. Fund raising. 2. Nonprofit organizations—Finance. I. Title.
  HG177.A343 2009
  658.15'224—dc22

                            2008053679

CONTENTS

1

Do You Need This Book?

Here's an easy test.

Let's pretend that a potential donor magically appears this instant and asks: *Why should I give you my money now?*

If you can persuasively answer that essential question and make the sale, you probably don't need this book.

But if you, like most, find yourself fumbling for answers, starting and restarting, feeling a bit like the proverbial "deer in the headlights" – then, yes, this book will definitely help you.

Seeing through a Donor's Eyes explains how to write a successful case for support. It guides you through the same step-by-step process I use to figure out and write cases for clients of all sizes and types. I've written dozens of cases. I have six underway as I type this sentence. Some are for capital campaigns. Some are for general support. And that brings up an issue.

■ Are cases just for capital campaigns? Heavens, no!

"I don't have a capital campaign," you might be thinking. "Why should I go to the bother of writing a case? I already have the case in my head."

Maybe you do. But consider....

- When you sit down to draft an appeal letter, does your wastebasket brim with discarded false starts, as you struggle to find a hook?

- When you plan the content for your newsletter, do you know exactly what kinds of stories to run?

- Do you know exactly what kinds of information donors need to find on your website?

- If you're invited to speak about your organization, do you know exactly which talking points are likely to lure supporters?

Writing a case helps you and your organization with all sorts of commonplace communication tasks.

The mere act of writing a case helps you – forces you, really – to deeply investigate your organization's impact on the world, so you can successfully explain that impact to donors and prospects.

Having a current case for support on file is an act of good management. A case consolidates your messages for common reference by staff and board, putting every potential voice, writer, and advocate on the same page.

To quote a higher authority, super-fundraiser Jerry Panas: "We almost always think of a Case Statement as an absolutely essential tool in preparing for a capital campaign. And it is. It is the *mother ship* of all other material. But note this. The Case Statement is just as important for ongoing annual giving. Just as important for planned giving. And for corporate gifts. And foundation grants. If you are interested in raising funds, your institution needs a current Case Statement. Period!"

2

And If You Are
in a Capital Campaign

*Why your volunteer solicitors will love
having in hand a good case for support*

In a recent article in the *Chronicle of Philanthropy*, Cedric Richner, a fundraising consultant, said, "Fear of asking for money is right up there with the fear of snakes and public speaking for many people."

Nerves, fear of failure, fear of rejection, uncertainty about one's ability to articulate, they all combine vilely in the volunteer's stomach.

A good case is an essential tool (and tranquilizer).

It acts as a loyal assistant, a ready reference. A well-reasoned, richly emotional case for support instills confidence in your volunteer solicitors like nothing else. It brings the campaign to life. It gives your perplexed, though brave, volunteer helpmates enough relevant talking points to make a meeting worthwhile and interesting.

I've known a disheartened board, doubtful of raising what they feared would be an insurmountable goal, break into relieved applause when they first saw the case for support. I kid you not.

Finally ... they knew what to say and how to say it. It inspired them to raise a record sum, incidentally, well past their original goal.

3

Types of Cases: A Shopping Guide

Stanley Weinstein, in his book, *Capital Campaigns from the Ground Up*, describes the thing thusly:

> "A case for support, also called a case statement, is a body of language that describes the rationale for supporting a nonprofit organization. It is written from the donor's perspective, primarily the desire to support worthwhile projects and organizations that help enhance the lives of others."

Every word in that synopsis is dead-on accurate. But I had to write a score of cases to realize it. "Body of language"? What in the world did *that* mean?

When I was new to cases and hungry for enlightenment *(please, Lord, don't let me fail to do my part in this multi-million dollar campaign)*, Stanley Weinstein's description and others like it (there must be a dozen books on the topic of capital campaigns) mystified me.

What does a case really look like? How do you use it? I was desperate to know about cases as *things*, not as concepts.

Here then, for your demystifying pleasure, is my guide to cases.

■ Internal case for support

The internal case is a collection of talking points – *all* the talking points that might somehow prove persuasive or informative when you communicate to prospects and donors.

Please note the special focus. The internal case for support has specific target audiences in mind: prospects, donors, and any others who might help your cause (reporters, for instance; or legislators, if you're an advocacy organization). The internal case is a database of messages. The League of Women Voters explains it this way:

"The internal case is a source document about your...vision, used in-house by the Board and staff. It gathers in one document pertinent and up-to-date information about your [organization]: its services, its unique qualities, its achievements, its plans, its reputation."

Exactly. As the League notes, an internal case is not a public document. It's not for prospects to see. It's not necessarily well written. My internal cases are full of "notes to self"; abbreviations; half-baked ideas I don't want to lose; references to other documents ("see page 5 of their annual report"); and other scribblings.

The internal case is also a place you can be refreshingly honest and frank ("We really do stink in this particular regard....") about your organization's worries ("Will we be here in 10 years?") and shortcomings ("We have six people doing the work of a baker's dozen. Yes, customer service is a problem.").

The internal case is strictly a parking lot. You drive in any information that you believe, feel, suspect, or hope might prove remotely useful in your fundraising communications.

Subsequently, down the road, you will refer to your internal case whenever you need things to say – in your appeal letters, feasibility cases, grant proposals, brochures, press pitches, editorials, PowerPoint presentations, website content, newsletter articles, and such.

Compiling an internal case – going to all the trouble (it *does* take a couple of days) – is a good thing to do every few years for *any* donor-dependent organization. I will personally stand behind that guarantee. And if you're attempting a capital or advocacy campaign, it *is* a must. The internal case fully maps your worthiness to supporters.

An internal case can be any length. I've had them as short as 1,000 words and as long as 20,000 words.

Tip: I bullet every item in my internal cases, and I **boldface** a key point in each item. This makes the material far easier to skim visually later, when I'm desperately trying to find that perfect quote or statistic I vaguely remember.

■ The general case for support

Every fundraising program needs a general case for support.

The general case summarizes why your mission matters. That's job #1. The general case also makes abundantly clear the essential role donors play in achieving that mission. That's job #2.

A general case for support answers the basic question: What makes our mission so urgent and worthy that it might win the financial support of someone with an interest in this cause?

The answer to that question influences what you say and show in normal (i.e., non-campaign) donor communications: your direct mail appeals, annual reports, website, emails, newsletter articles, presentations and so on.

A general case can be relatively brief; some are fewer than 100 words. On the next page is one for a sciences program at a state university:

Right now, the fate of our planet can seem desperately unsure. You might well wonder: Has our industrial past poisoned our future? Take hope. Here, in our university's laboratories, world-class scientists (three Nobel laureates) and engineers (we have one of the best engineering schools on the planet says *The Economist*) are creating an exciting new future that will fix some of the world's most urgent problems. But we can't get there without your help. We depend on donor support every year. Your help is crucial.

"Could the donor read this just the way it is?" you might ask. Possibly. It's not badly written. But its real purpose is to clarify the basic message, so that everything said or sent sings the same tune, over and over. Here's another general case to help you get the idea, this for a youth mental health organization:

Safety net. That's one way to describe us. Ask a family who's come to us for counseling, desperate for one small ray of hope. Or someone we've brought along from homeless teen to self-sufficient young adult. Or parents worried about drug use after school, a tragedy we now see in our community as early as the elementary grades. We can do something about all these crises. But only with your continued support. Every year, to meet the needs of local families and youth, we have to raise a half-million dollars from donors like you.

One last provocation: if you haven't written a general case for support recently, I'd wager you really don't know why you're raising money. Writing a general case forces you to think about your organization's promise, your organization's proof, and how the donor fits into your world.

A hospital (in this award-winning effort by Southcoast's in-house marketing group) reduces its case for a new emergency department to a single thrilling/chilling word (*Urgent*) and an action photo. This case was used during both the quiet phase and the public phase for a campaign that exceeded goal.

■ Cases for the quiet period of a capital campaign: Feasibility and draft

Compton, a consulting firm with more than 1,000 capital campaigns under its belt, says you'll raise 80 percent of your goal from 100 to 150 people. That estimate is probably conservative. Senior fundraisers I've interviewed insist that "97 percent of your goal comes from 3 percent of the donors."

Translation: *It's face-to-face solicitations, baby.* Count on it.

There is no alternative, according to Compton: "Letter writing, house-to-house collections, events and other run-of-the-mill fundraising will simply not raise enough money" to meet "a major, fundraising need."

Therefore, you *will* be talking first to your best prospects. Peer-to-peer solicitations are the rule.

Let's not be naive: exclusivity (a powerful emotional trigger) is part of the charm. Only a relative handful of people (maybe 5,000 individuals during a billion-dollar campaign; equivalent to about 8 percent of the donors) will be asked to share your dreams. They will know *before the rest of the world* exactly what your vision is. They'll be insiders. If they give, they will join a very select group of early investors. They'll become visionaries themselves.

This is called the "quiet" period. Sometimes the quiet period also includes a feasibility study. During the feasibility study (also known as a "resources study") you (the organization) are asking basic questions of high-value prospects: *Would our proposed project interest you enough to merit a gift? If not, why not?*

During the quiet period – whether you're already fundraising or still determining your project's philanthropic feasibility – a lucid, well-organized Word document will suffice.

Some organizations leap right to a fancy, printed case. I don't oppose that leap. Since I write exactly those kinds of fancy-pants cases, I'm happy to pocket the fees.

But, be fair, do you really need a splashy case during the quiet period? Likely not. At this stage, the information matters far more than the glitz.

Jerry Panas likes to stamp DRAFT in bold red letters on the cover of his quiet-phase cases. They're no more than lightly illustrated Word documents at this stage.

Trumpeting DRAFT, in red, reinforces among your prospects the gratifying notion that the project remains open to ideas and opinions. Your prospects, i.e., can contribute thoughts as well as cash.

People hope you appreciate them for their intelligence as much as for their bank balance – as the emergency-red word DRAFT implies. Flattery is a predictably powerful and persuasive emotional trigger.

■ The public case for a capital campaign

After the quiet phase comes the public phase of your capital campaign. Now – finally – you're telling the world. The public phase is the "retail" part of your campaign. You have the remaining portion of your goal to raise.

Retail fundraising requires mass communications. The University of Toronto recently raised $1 billion. It took seven years. It took 112,819 donors to make goal.

For your campaign, expect to inform thousands of prospects about your vision. During the public phase of a capital campaign you'll probably need a printed brochure, to reach that many.

4

Why You Matter to Donors

A case for support, in my opinion, is not very much about what your organization *does*: the daily activities, how it works, the operating hours, the staff, the names of programs, and a thousand other mundane details.

I believe a case is mostly about your *promise*, the promise you make to the world through your mission, your accomplishments, and your plans. Call it "the big picture."

Last year, Maureen Welch, then at the Antiquarian and Landmarks Society in Connecticut, sent a plea. She asked me to consider writing a book titled *Who are you kidding: Help for non-essential nonprofits*.

Her suggestion was a jest. But not entirely. There are plenty of nonprofits who suspect they're in a similar fix: nice but non-essential; and therefore not very compelling or competitive in the philanthropic marketplace.

The Society (which has changed its name to Connecticut Landmarks) is a first-rate outfit. It manages, preserves, and opens to the public a distinguished portfolio of magnificent old homes dating as far back as 1678. They are lovely relics. Still, Maureen found it hard to imagine what case for support she could propose that would tug at donors' heart strings like charities can that improve the world or ease suffering. Maureen, this chapter's for you.

■ There's no such thing as a generic "donor"

Trust me, "non-essential" charities, you have your donors. You just have to find them. Will you find thousands? Perhaps not; not every charity has mass-market appeal. But there are certainly people out there who share your interests.

People seldom give to a charity by mistake. They're likely to give because a charity's mission has personal meaning for them. A short list:

• They want to give back. "I had no idea what to do with myself as a kid. But college opened up a wide new world. It's been a good life since."

• They have special interests. "I love hiking these woods. It makes me feel twice as alive!"

• They have cherished priorities. "I saw my father die from that disease. I'm going to help until they find a cure."

• They have firm beliefs. "It's the art and the artists that make this city an exciting place to live."

• They have experiences and memories. "A mentor at the right time changed my life more than once. Everybody should be so lucky."

• They have values. "Every child deserves a shot at a good education."

Take me, for instance. Could the Antiquarian and Landmarks Society land me as a donor?

It depends. One thing definitely works against them in my particular case: I don't live in Connecticut. And people do like to give locally where they can see (and even experience) the results themselves.

Still, like lots of people, I value history. I read history books for pleasure – and to gain perspective on current affairs.

To my history-loving eyes, therefore, the Society's work is not that much about saving buildings from ruin. That *is* the fundamental activity, sure. But that's not why the Society might matter to me.

And here we come to a nub.

■ You matter – but maybe not for the reason you think

You might think your mission is one thing while your donors feel it's something else.

The Society describes itself this way on its website as of this writing: "Founded in 1936, our mission is to inspire appreciation for the Connecticut experience by preserving, presenting and promoting outstanding historical properties."

Not a bad nutshell. But does it reflect a donor's interests? You have to wonder what it means "to inspire appreciation for the Connecticut experience." Outside the state, not that much. There's a Connecticut experience. There's a Utah experience. There are 48 other state experiences.

And inside the state? The Connecticut experience, judging superficially by the Society's inventory of upper-caste buildings, appears to be an only-the-wealthy-need-apply kind of thing.

I'm not trying to pick on the Society. Honestly, visitors would rather look at extraordinary houses than ordinary houses any day. The Society's board and staff do excellent work in a tough donor environment. They gorgeously maintain the structures in their care. And they develop innovative programming to attract new audiences.

My point is merely this: you might want to write *two* mission statements. One, the in-house one, serves as a rudder for the board and staff. The second should be relevant to donors.

■ The donor-specific mission statement

Organizations are chronically unable to distinguish between activities and accomplishments. This leads to no end of trouble.

The Antiquarian and Landmarks Society, for example, knows to the penny all the time and treasure that goes into maintaining its stellar collection of properties. So the Society assumes preservation is its primary mission (and lists that item first in its mission). That's the insider's point of view.

But outsiders' (i.e., donors') points of view are different. They derive from an array of personal interests:

• I might be into house restoration myself, for instance, and be interested in construction techniques of a certain period.

• I might collect antiques and be interested in the milieu, when today's antiques were objects in everyday use.

• I might have an interest in local history because of my family origins.

• I might be a set designer interesting in period interiors for a play.

• I might have an affectionate interest in a certain period in history that a particular house represents.

And so on. Buildings preserve more than bricks, boards, and furnishings; they preserve the ways of life lived in them, the tools employed to build them, the struggles of their eras: human history, in other words...and all the things that history does for us (entertain, inform, lend perspective, shock, surprise, remind).

Each building preserved by the Society is a time machine. It can authentically take us to a different period. And without the Society, these increasingly rare time portals won't survive. And without donors, the Society won't survive. That's how slender is the thread on which authentic history hangs.

Historic buildings are endangered species by another name; there are fewer of them left every year. Dr. Robert Cialdini, author of *The New York Times* business best seller, *Influence: The Psychology of Persuasion,* spotlights what he calls the "scarcity" principle. It's one of his "six most fundamental principles of influence." In fundraising it goes something like this: if you tell me something I value is in danger of disappearing, I will instinctively want to save it. An appeal that talks about what I stand to lose is even more powerful than an appeal that talks about what I stand to gain, his research shows.

A donor mission statement for the Society might well begin, "Without the Society and the donors who stand behind it, these one-of-a-kind historical treasures – and the lessons they continue to teach us about our world and theirs – will be lost forever."

Now that's an emotional pitch even a Rhode Islander like myself can relate to.

■ An essential exercise for non-essential nonprofits: "What if we disappeared tonight?"

The following is an exercise I strongly recommend for *all* nonprofits, whether they suffer from "non-essential-itis" or not.

This dirt-simple but deeply revealing exercise forces you to zero in on why your organization and its activities really matter to outsiders. Guaranteed: the fresh perspectives you uncover will help you create fundraising communications that are far more persuasive.

Here's what you do.

Gather a half-dozen or more stakeholders in a room: staff; board; donors, too, if you can. Pose this problem: *Let's pretend. Let's pretend our organization and its programs disappear tonight. Tomorrow, we're gone. What will the world/the community/individuals regret having lost?*

This is not a make-work exercise. This is a core exercise. Attendees in my workshops who try this exercise for even a few minutes are shocked, surprised, and then empowered by what they discover about their organization's true importance and impact.

In their business bestseller, *Made to Stick*, Chip and Dan Heath warn organizations against the "curse of knowledge": the creeping inability of insiders to see themselves the way outsiders (e.g., donors with all their many values, concerns, interests, and connections) do.

The curse turns nonprofits irrelevant. They talk about things that do not matter, in ways that do not persuade. Going through the exercise of asking – *If we were to disappear tonight, what would the world shed tears over losing?* – helps break the curse of knowledge and gives you well-grounded answers to that most important of questions: *Why would a donor care about the things we do?*

5

Writing a Fabulous Case is Easy

You're just answering questions

To write a great case, you take on a new job title. You become the Designated Stranger. You pretend you know nothing about your organization. And you ask yourself the kinds of basic, skeptical, questions that outsiders tend to have.

What kinds of questions will a prospective donor have? Nothing outlandish:

- Why is your mission/plan/program so vital?
- Why is your solution so good/proven/unique?
- Why is now so urgent?
- Why do you need donors at all?

Here's how Yale president, Richard C. Levin, opens his case for the university's Tomorrow campaign. The first paragraph is nothing but answers to basic questions:

> I invite you to participate in Yale Tomorrow **[question #1: Why am I contacting you?]**, a five-year, $3 billion campaign **[question #2: What is the scope of the campaign?]** to build the future of our university **[question #3: Why does the campaign matter to the institution?]**. I seek your support to

ensure that the accomplishment of recent years is not remembered merely as a bright moment in Yale's long history **[question #4: What is the urgent problem that drives the campaign?]**, but rather as the foundation for a Yale of permanently greater breadth and strength, a Yale with the capacity to contribute—by means of its scholarship and its graduates—not only to the nation but also to the world **[question #5: What is the promise of the campaign?]**.

■ Answering special questions

Your case might have to answer some unique questions, too; questions that only apply to your special situation.

Yale, for instance, as I write this, has the second largest academic endowment on the face of the earth; the sum is vast and well advertised. Which leads to an obvious question: "If Yale is already unimaginably rich, why, President Levin, do you need yet more of my money?" His second paragraph hurries to explain:

Even our most loyal supporters might wonder, after examining the spectacular performance of our Investments Office these past two decades, whether Yale needs to augment still further its already abundant financial resources. It is important to recognize that most of our existing endowment funds were given by donors of the past and present to be used for specifically designated purposes. Thus, most of our endowment provides a strong foundation for our current activities, while the relatively small fraction of the endowment that is unrestricted permits only limited scope for innovation.

In other words, Yale needs more unrestricted money or its "scope for innovation" will be "limited."

Let me give you one other example of answering an obvious

question.

When the Rhode Island Philharmonic launched a capital campaign to retire its structural deficit, the organization knew that people would ask:

1) Isn't a deficit a *bad* thing, a sign that your management lacks business sense?

2) And, hey, if the orchestra needs money, why don't you just raise ticket prices, like any for-profit would?

So the Philharmonic's printed case opened with the frank statement: "A symphony is a tough business. Every time you perform, you lose money ... if you depend on ticket sales alone."

The case then revealed that all the very best symphonies had structural deficits. The Boston Symphony did, the National Symphony did, the Philadelphia Orchestra did.

A structural deficit, the case argued, had in fact become something of an *indicator* among U.S. symphonies of top-tier musicianship. Truth to tell, the case argued, if your symphony *didn't* have a structural deficit, maybe you (Dear Live Classical Music Lover and Potential Supporter) should wonder *why not*. After all, top professional musicians, interesting conductors, acoustically perfect performance venues, and celebrity guest soloists do cost serious money.

It was such a persuasive case that the Tucson Symphony fielded pretty much the same argument during its Prelude campaign. In Tucson's version:

> A structural deficit is a badge of quality in the world of live symphonic music. All the best orchestras have one.
>
> Not that they want to, mind you. But even sky-high ticket prices don't begin to cover the cost of a modern professional orchestra.
>
> It's a tough business playing Classical music at a level people

want to hear. Every time you perform, you lose money ... if you depend on ticket sales alone.

Consider the National Symphony, resident at the Kennedy Center in Washington, DC. The National Symphony earns just 60 percent of its income from ticket sales. And that's pretty typical across the US. To balance the books, you need other sources of income. What's the most important other source?

A permanent endowment.

Every self-respecting orchestra needs one.

An adequate endowment can do amazing things. The mighty Boston Symphony Orchestra pockets $6 million a year in income from its endowment. We don't need as much as the BSO by a long shot. But we do need to make our current endowment at least 10 times bigger to cover our anticipated costs and mend TSO's structural deficit woes.

By anticipating their donors' thorniest question – and offering a well-researched and reasonable answer up front, these orchestras put to rest a potentially serious objection and turned what was their campaigns' biggest negative into a reassuring positive.

6

The Case Writing Process: An Overview

Left to my own devices, without any other work to do, with all my interviewees immediately available, and lacking any need for anyone's approval or review, it takes me, start to finish, about a week to write a case for support.

That's not the real world, of course. That's just the raw time requirement – in a perfect, no problems, world. In real life, in real time, with normal delays, and the usual fuss-widget approval process, the work often spins out like a long, lazy summer.

If you get your case done within three months, you've earned the nickname "speedy"; you're probably beating the average. If it takes you six months to complete a case, you're about typical.

On rare occasions (been there, done that) the case *never* reaches closure; it just fades away. Alas. Things happen: the feasibility study reports discouraging news, the details of the project change, the executive director retires, a major matching gift fails to materialize, the organization switches direction, or approval turns into a morass.

In a perfect world, though, here are the steps:

• Day one: You assemble your background materials.·

• Day two: You conduct your key informant interviews.

• Day three: You skim the cream from your backgrounders and your interviews.

• Day four: You write the internal case. (You can stop here if you're not conducting a capital campaign. An internal case is sufficient as a base for an annual fundraising program.)

• Days five through seven: You write the external case.

If you're publishing a nicely printed case statement, you'll also have to add time for photography, graphic design, and printing. As a rule of thumb, I allot at least two months to accommodate designers and printers. All things considered, if you begin your case in January and have in hand a printed piece by September, you're probably doing better than many.

7

Day 1:
Gather Your Pile
of Information

On day one you gather your background materials. What's needed will vary.

For a child and family service agency serving a six-town area, the background materials that yielded tidbits of worthwhile information were:

- The budget for the current fiscal year (which demonstrated how heavily the agency relied on charitable dollars)
- The two most recent annual reports (which talked about activities and service statistics)
- An organizational profile that covered mission, history, goals, challenges, accomplishments, current programs, and marketplace (i.e., competing service providers)
- Six brief testimonials: from a parent, a school principal, and various teens·
- An agency brochure
- One gift-solicitation letter

On my desk: the background materials for a university's case. In a sprawling case for support, you could end up reviewing a book's worth of information to find a few nuggets of gold. Your job is to reduce that mountain down to a final reader-ready case of 1,500-4,500 well-chosen words.

• Notes from the agency's strategic planning process, where board members talked about the agency's plans

On the other hand, for an advocacy campaign that won passage of a $50 million bond to build affordable housing, the background materials filled a large box and included:

• More than 60 documents, drawn from dozens of credible sources, including information on trends, case studies of effective advocacy happening elsewhere, editorials, economic analyses, briefings on zoning and construction innovations.

• A book about messaging against determined foes: George Lakoff's *Don't Think of an Elephant.*

• Phone conversations with other states who'd attempted similar things.

• Interviews with 25 "stakeholders," from grassroots organizers to builders to town officials to the state's senate policy office.

As you think about what kinds of background materials you might want to collect and review for your case, use the following as a checklist of possibilities.

Background materials about the fundamentals: who you are and why you matter

- Your mission
- Your values
- Organization's history
- Data on those you serve
- Your position papers
- Your letters to the editor
- Your board

Background materials about what you do

- Your press releases
- Recent outbound communications (your newsletters, for instance)
- Descriptions of your programs and services (brochures and catalogs)
- Proof your programs work
- Staff profiles
- Financial information
- Case studies or anecdotes of individuals you've helped
- Event calendars

Background materials on where you're headed

- Your vision
- Your strategic plan (goals and objectives)

• Your campaign's monetary goal and what that money buys

• Articles on trends that will impact your organization (for example, the surging impact that aging Baby Boomers are having on health care; or the proliferation of non-English native languages in America's inner-city classrooms)

Background materials on how others see you

• News clippings about you (reporters are outsiders; they often do the best job of summing up who you are and why you matter, from the public's view)

• Testimonials (Jerry Weissman, author of *Presenting to Win*, says "you need to move the dubious audience to believe." Nothing I know converts skeptics into believers faster than a positive testimonial from a credible source.)

• Rankings (how *US News & World Report* ranks your university, for instance; or where the National Research Council's latest study ranks your faculty's performance)

• Awards

One last tip: Search online for other cases and steal anything that seems good and convincing.

Did I know everything there was to know about endowed chairs the first time a college hired me to write that particular kind of case? Sure: *after* I'd Googled the key words "endowed chair campaign" and invested a few well-spent hours online, poring over a dozen cases from other schools and lifting their best arguments.

Looking at other cases is reassuring, too. You might stumble on one or two that are brilliant. Most aren't. You'll see that writing a case is well within reach, even if you're a novice.

8

Also on Day 1: Decide about Interviews

Anthropologists call them "key informants," and they are vital.

They are true insiders. In anthropology, they are knowledgeable natives who help a visiting researcher understand how the local culture really works: the bloodlines, the politics, the hidden meanings.

In fundraising, a key informant is someone whose opinion and special knowledge will help you build your case.

Who are they? People with vision (maybe your executive director). People who know the best stories about how your organization changes lives and the world (maybe your program staff). People who know why donors love you (pick any long-time donor).

Figure out your key informants and schedule interviews with them.

■ Interview as few as possible

Keep in mind that each interview you conduct could consume three hours of your precious time: for preparation (to ask intelligent questions); for the interview itself; and for review and mark-up of your interview notes.

I've conducted hundreds of interviews. Three hours apiece is not a wild guess. At that rate, if you schedule 30 interviews, you could be facing a cumulative 90 hours of work. Who has that kind of time?

So, when drawing up your list of interviewees, try to be exclusive. Ask yourself: "If I could only interview one person, who would that be?" Who do you think has the best knowledge of the program, the cagiest insights, the strongest emotions about the vision?

Of course, one interview is seldom enough. Internal politics often play a role. "If you're talking to Sally, then you *have* to talk to Joe." And anything to do with higher ed, expect to talk to a lot of people. Colleges pride themselves on consensus, so every opinion gets a hearing. My personal campus record, set recently, is 23 interviews in a day and a half.

Truth be told, though, most cases for support, in the end, hang off the insights of relatively few interviewees. Unfortunately, you won't know who these "super-informants" are in advance. Prepare to interview more than you need.

■ Who's on your key informant list? A few actual cases.

• For a campaign **to build a new emergency department at a community hospital**, two hours spent with the front-line nurses and doctors provided more than enough sizzle and steak to sell the project. Focus groups with community members (another way to interview key informants) supplied important insights regarding the hospital's reputation.

• For a campaign **to endow 19 university chairs**, I interviewed a dozen academicians. Roll call included the president, the dean of the faculty, five department heads, the head of advancement, and senior VPs from administration.

The dean of the faculty and the department heads gave me most of the substance for the case. They were front-line people; they themselves taught and researched; they knew the students. They could vividly imagine what kinds of intriguing minds would occupy these competitive chairs and the intellectual fireworks that would ensue. The administration suits had little to offer beyond platitudes.

• For a **$300 million all-purpose capital campaign at a public research university**, I spoke with a dozen individuals, mostly high-ranking academics.

Four cracked the case for me: the deans of the undergraduate and graduate schools (both highly ambitious individuals; the ambitious are always great to talk to); the newly hired executive in charge of admissions; and an alumnus. The alum had returned after two decades to what he remembered as a pretty nondescript school and stood astonished by the impressive achievements he saw on every hand.

• To find **the right messaging for a successful $50 million bond campaign**, I interviewed two dozen stakeholders. Of that group, just three interviews cracked the case for me. But that's hindsight talking. In advance I couldn't have predicted who would have the right answers.

• At the other end of the scale, for a small Jewish family service agency on a tight budget that needed a case **for its overall fundraising program**, I interviewed exactly one person: the executive director. He had his hands in everything. Plus I read a few of the agency's very good newsletters. A few hours later the agency's four-page case for support was finished.

9

Day 2: Conduct Your Interviews

Take copious notes. Beware GIGO

On day one you gathered your pile of background information. You also decided on and scheduled interviews. Next step: interviewing those key informants.

Once you finish your interviews, by the way, you're done with the research phase of creating your case for support; and you can move on to the concept phase.

■ How to interview

I've interviewed hundreds of key informants. Most of those interviews lasted 45 minutes or less. I come prepared with a starter question or two, then we see where the conversation takes us. I nod and make encouraging noises. But mostly I stay quiet. In a 45-minute interview, I'll talk for maybe three minutes, five minutes tops. What I do instead is scribble copious notes.

If you were reading over my shoulder while I interview, you'd see that I'm not capturing every word, though. My notes are pretty sketchy. I'm looking for ideas, facts and opinions.

If I do happen to hear a good sound bite, I'll write that down more or less verbatim. Very rarely (once in a hundred interviews) I will bring a voice recorder, mostly if I'll be speaking to someone – let's say a research scientist – whose information could be technically beyond my immediate grasp. The recording device lets me relax during the interview; I won't miss a precious word.

You might think it's easier to sit back and let a voice recorder do the work. But you're simply postponing the pain. Eventually, you will have to either transcribe the interview or make written notes. I get that pain out of the way during the interview by making my written notes as I go, even on those rare occasions when I'm recording.

You can interview in person. You can interview by phone. My interviews are half one and half the other. The advantage of interviewing in person, of course, is the chance to look around and see things. When a zoo wants to raise $35 million for renovations, the interview with the executive director takes place as we walk from exhibit to exhibit, through the behind-the-scenes enclosures (watch where you step; elephant dung is as deep as a pillow). I'm taking notes on the smells, sights and sounds as well as the ED's conversation.

■ Interviews put you outside your known world

You might be thinking: *Why do I need to do* any *interviews? I already know our organization inside and out.*

That's your problem right there: you *do* know it too well. Or a piece of it anyway.[1]

"The curse of knowledge," the Heath brothers call it in their business best-seller, *Made to Stick*.

---

[1] And don't be too smug about the piece you do know. I double-check every "fact" insiders tell me. A surprising number prove to be wrong, distorted, or missing the point.

"Lots of research in economics and psychology," they said in an interview, "shows that when we know something, it becomes hard for us to imagine not knowing it. As a result, we become lousy communicators."

We inflict a towering Babel of "insider" lingo on our audiences: social-worker-speak, education-ese, church talk. Community foundations choke on specialist terminology: permanent endowment, unrestricted funds, designated funds, field of interest funds, professional advisors, donor advisors, the philanthropic services group, the program staff. Words like these are a wall. They keep people away.

I am always an outsider. I *have* to do interviews to immerse myself in a client's story. But remember your new job title: Designated Stranger. As the Designated Stranger, you're seeking to understand your organization in a way no one else in your organization does: through a donor's heart and mind.

When you interview, you need to become a surrogate for the donor. You need to experience wonder reborn. Super-presenter, Jerry Weissman, calls this Audience Advocacy: "...learning to view yourself, your company, your story, and your presentation through the eyes of your audience."

Become a blank slate. Forget office politics. Pretend you don't know your organization's full story yet.

And when you interview someone else on staff, ask "stupid" questions like "Why do we it that way, anyway?" I predict you'll be surprised by what you learn.

■ As for interviews: Garbage in, garbage out

It's a saying (and an acronym: GIGO) from the early days of computing: garbage in, garbage out. Translation: the system's not to blame – if you enter bad data, expect poor results.

Things you hear during interviews can mislead you. Here are two common GIGOs to watch out for:

1) It's the truth, just not a palatable truth for an outside audience.

My sole key informant, a vice president of finance, told me the bald truth, as he knew it: traditional funding was down sharply. Time and budget allowed for just one interview; he was it.

Deficits had city government reeling, he sighed. A scandal-tainted United Way was a shadow of its former self, he lamented. Both had deeply sliced their funding in recent years, costing his child and family service agency millions of dollars in lost revenue. Which in turn threatened the continuation of three core programs.

I dutifully donned my best worried expression and wrote a case about a "rescue": a campaign to raise a multi-million dollar endowment to guarantee the programs' survival.

The executive director was appalled when she read it. "This makes it sound like we're going out of business!"

GIGO strikes again. By limiting ourselves to a single interview, I got a keyhole view, not a full view. While some programs *were* on the brink, as my informant had said, other programs were doing fine and the agency's overall health was good. In the executive director's view, my "rescue" idea threatened to paint the entire agency with a gloomy brush that only applied to three programs.

It was an easy fix. I wrote a second case, keeping her reaction in mind. This time we called it "The Campaign to Reach More." My "rescue" case had proposed a glass half empty, in danger of drying up. The "Campaign to Reach More" described a glass half full; prepared to brim, if donors could be found. Same agency, same problem; different point of view.

2) You're selling something. You're just not sure what.

If you get three drafts into a case, and the boss says you still haven't nailed it, it's time to ask, with all due respect, *Do we really know what we're selling? And whom we're selling it to?*

I'm hired. I interview the college president by phone. I write a well-reasoned, emotionally satisfying case based on his comments. And I hear back, via the director of advancement: *Sorry, no. There's something missing.*

So I fly to the college and interview a flock of new key informants. I write a well-reasoned, emotionally satisfying case based on their comments, taking a new angle suggested by the president. And hear for a second time: *Sorry. It's still not quite right.*

This time, since we're all suffering from near-terminal frustration, my client prepares an in-depth outline of the case for me to follow. I cling to the outline desperately. With renewed confidence, I present my third draft – a well-reasoned, emotionally satisfying case richly supported by key informant quotes – only to hear once more (and for the last time; I'd fire me, too, at this point): *Umm ... sorry, the president just doesn't like it.*

What went wrong? Garden variety GIGO, in my opinion. Call it, "The Case of the Premature Case."

The capital campaign was for a $45 million academic building, the first new classroom structure in decades. But the details were still in flux. The architect had nothing on paper. The school hoped to talk instead about what the building would mean to students and the world.

Which can be an engaging, persuasive strategy. The *promise* of a building excites the reader's mind, maybe more than the building itself. Just imagine all the ideas and careers waiting to take wing inside its classrooms. It's the "sky's the limit" approach.

But there was no real consensus on the promise, either. The college had a new president, still choosing his talking points. His point of attack shifted each time we spoke. The planning committee was an all-star team, a host of bright minds – with an equal number of opinions. Adding insult to injury, the school's sense of self was dangerously humble. The college wanted its new building to be something great – yet didn't dare speak the words, for fear of offending a "militantly modest" alumni base.

As I said: premature.

If you don't really know what you're selling, and you haven't yet talked to your best prospects about the project, you are in deep GIGO. Don't expect to write an articulate case if you're still doing your homework.

10

What Kinds of Interview Questions?

Organizations have their needs: a new boiler, replace the roof, repairs to this or that. Desperately needed? Absolutely. Inspiring to donors? Not exactly.

During your interviews, ask simple little questions, dumb-seeming even. Don't settle for the obvious: "We need a new boiler."

Why do you need a new boiler? "Because the old one keeps breaking down."

So you need a reliable boiler. Why is that so important? "Because we always need hot water when the kids we're trying to help come out here to the farm. And at least six months out of the year we've got the heat on."

Okay. So kids can't come here if you don't have a reliable boiler. But why does coming here matter so much to those kids? "Because there are kids who never smile – except when they are here."

Hold it.

Now *that's* a statement that might inspire a donor. Case writer Brigitte C. Mertling unearthed that comment deep into her interviews with a nonprofit that runs a fully accessible farm. The farm gives people with disabilities a chance to feed and mingle with animals.

And that's exactly what donors want to hear about: smiles. For donors, the boiler you need is not the point. The real point – the thing that inspires – is that rare smile exploding across a disabled child's face when he's licked by a cow. That smile is emotional gold. You want a boiler? Write about an exploding smile.

You will always get an answer if you ask a question. But it will be an automatic, obvious answer. Don't stop there. Ask why. Don't accept everything you hear at face value, because it's usually only part of the story. Learn to probe.

■ Envisioning questions

Bringing something new into the world, as a capital campaign often aims to do, is an act of imagination. You're asking donors to purchase something they can't yet see or touch.

Your interviewees can help you bring the vision to life if you ask them "envisioning" questions. These kinds of questions create mental pictures. Here are some real-life examples:

For an endowed chairs campaign: "What kind of scholar do you see recruiting for this chair? Who is it? What did they do that was so great?"

For a youth services agency: "What frightens you most about where these kids could end up in a few years?"

For anyone: "What happens if you don't get the money?"

It's fun to speculate. Put your interviewees in a time machine for a moment: send them a few years forward. Ask them to report back on the changes they see.

Other questions worth asking a key informant inside the organization:

• What catalyst or big event or realization led us to this particular program, project, or mission?

• If we had to reduce our work to just one program, which would it be and why?

• What is pinching the organization now? What prevents the organization from doing more good in the world?

• Is there a crisis brewing? Will we face a showdown with some obstacle in the foreseeable future?

• If the organization had all the money in the world, what would we do?

• What comes next? Not just tomorrow, but the day *after* tomorrow?

• What does hope look like for the people we serve?

• What does fear look like for the people we serve?

• What values do our donors have? (For instance, what would delight our donors?)

• What concerns do our donors have? (For instance, what makes our donors angry?)

• What special interests do our donors have?

• Do you have a story about the people we help that perfectly illustrates why this program, project, or mission matters?

11

Day 3: Skim the Cream

At this point in the process you have raked together a large pile of research. It includes everything from your agency's newsletters to your interview notes.

Now it's time to find the brightest needles in your haystack and put aside the rest. It's a matter, really, of turning 50,000 words (or more) into 5,000 words (or less), all of it relevant to your donors' interests.

I love this day. I can do it anywhere. It doesn't require a computer at hand. Your basic tools are a highlighter and Post-it® notes. I like to sit in the garden with my stack of background information, listening to music on headphones, with a pen nearby for making quick notes.

■ Be ruthlessly picky

On day two, when you collected your research, you were inclusive. Today you will be rigidly *exclusive*: you're poking through your material, looking for only the very best – tidbits; anecdotes; sound bites; testimonials; statistical data; clear proof that your mission matters, that your solution works; powerful emotional hooks; surprising news; big predictions.

• You have 25 statistics? Pick ONE as the best ... because it vividly reveals something worth knowing: a trend, a shame, a threat, or an

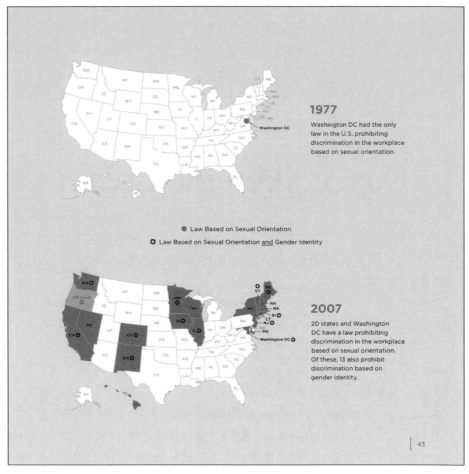

Admirable concision: NCLR summarized progress on a key national issue with two maps and a few words. Design: Orange Square.

opportunity to change things for the better.

• You have a dozen testimonials? Pick the three juiciest … ones that make a point, that depict you as effective, that reveal the promise of your plan.

• Look for what's new. The human mind involuntarily responds to anything new in its environment, whether that thing is important or not. Keep feeding our brains bits of news, and we'll continue paying attention.

• Look for what's unique about your programs or ideas. Donors prefer to give to the unique. It's Advertising Psychology 101. What are you doing that others don't/can't/won't? Why are your methods uniquely important? Ditto: your vision.

• Look for what's dramatic. That's often a story of some kind, maybe a tale of how your mission changed someone's life, maybe a tale of some stunning discovery.

• Look for accomplishments. Donors want to make a real difference with their gifts. Effective charities with proven results are far more attractive.

Never forget that ultimately you will be explaining your case to a prospect who is volunteering their time – and maybe their money, if they buy what you're offering. Don't pad your case with second-rate information. It wastes everyone's time. Be an information snob: only include the very best.

12

Wanted: Emotional Triggers and Benefits

One of the things to figure out when you're throwing together your internal case is the emotional side of things. Ask yourself as you look through the items you're including and sorting, "Which emotions might this be able to stir in my prospects?"

Prospects want to be moved. I mean hearts-beating-faster moved ... hairs-standing-on-end moved ... levitation-moved: lifted right out of their seats — as they read what you have to say.

It seldom happens.

In many cases, every phrase is predictable. And nothing moves you. In fact, nothing even tries to move you. The case says little more than: "We do good work. We'll tell you how. Give us money." Intellectually, you understand the pitch, sure. But are you moved? No.

Don't be afraid to open your heart wide when you're writing your case.

We're not fundraisers so much as "hope-raisers," really. You are a *merchant* of hope. You're selling to donors the credible hope that they can change the world for the better ... through you ... if they invest in your merry band of troublemakers, change agents, teachers, healers, saints or such.

■ The emotional imperative

All decisions (the decision to make a gift, for instance) have emotional roots, neuroscience now knows.

We believe otherwise. Our minds have run a lifelong scam, convincing us that we are rational beings who carefully weigh the consequences of each choice. We treasure logic, we tell ourselves. It defines us.

That theory is about as right as the long-ago certainty that the world was flat.

Scientists can now watch the brain at work, thanks to advanced diagnostic tools like MRIs. And the truth is out: rational decisions have emotional origins. And not just some of the time. Leading researcher Dr. Antonio Damasio: "...even with what we believe are logical decisions, the very point of choice is arguably always based on emotion."

Using emotion in persuasion "is not an illicit appeal to irrationality, as Enlightenment thought would have it," argues cognitive scientist George Lakoff in his book *The Political Mind*. "The proper emotions are rational. It is rational to be outraged by torture, or by corruption, or by character assassination, or by lies that lead to thousands of deaths. If your policies will make people happy, then arousing hope and joy is rational. If the earth itself is in imminent danger, fear is rational."

Lakoff makes another point in favor of emotionally-based appeals: "...what most people are not aware of, and are sometimes shocked to discover, is that most of our thought – an estimated 98 percent – is

The key words here? "On the Brink." This newsletter headline uses loss (and its prevention) to underline the urgent importance of the Audubon Society of Rhode Island's work.

not conscious. [It is] automatic, uncontrolled."

Emotions come in many colors: hope, joy, greed, anger, flattery, and salvation to name just a tiny few.

Emotional triggers like "a desire to give back" (behind every alumni campaign) and "the urge to forestall loss" (behind every environmental protection cause) are the great hydroelectric dams of fundraising: they power countless organizations.

Think of the human heart as a bell.

You're trying to ring that bell repeatedly. Ding, ding, ding. Soft, sweet, nice.

And the little bell-ringing hammers are the emotional triggers you include in your case.

■ Greed considered

There is good greed. Would Michael Douglas say it if it weren't true? In his Oscar-winning role as corporate raider Gordon Gekko in the 1987 film *Wall Street*, he insists:

> "The point is, ladies and gentlemen, that greed – for lack of a better word – is good. Greed is right. Greed works. Greed clarifies, cuts through, and captures the essence of the evolutionary spirit. Greed, in all of its forms – greed for life, for money, for love, knowledge – has marked the upward surge of mankind. And greed – you mark my words – will not only save Teldar Paper, but that other malfunctioning corporation called the USA."

First of all, excellent job, Mr. Gekko, in making your case *bigger*.

Second, Gordon Gekko is fundamentally right: greed gets us all sorts of things we wouldn't have in our lives otherwise.

Greed for lengthier, healthier lives funds medical miracles. Greed for more productive, more satisfying lives funds education. Greed for a sustainable planet funds the environmental movement.

Selfish greed might be a bad thing; I'm not qualified to say. But *unselfish* greed, the kind that makes up philanthropy, is wonderful for the world.

■ Benefits: What they look like in a case

In the world of advertising, greed has a special voice. It's called speaking in benefits rather than in features. A feature is what you *do*. A benefit is why that thing *matters*. This is a feature: *We operate a 24-hour hot line*. This is the benefit of that feature: *Because crises don't happen on a 9-to-5 basis*.

The following passage opens the case for the French-American

School of Rhode Island. The passage is flush with benefits:

We admit it, we're odd: a school in Providence accredited by both the French government and the Rhode Island Board of Education. And here we do an odd thing, otherwise almost unobtainable in our region **[benefit #1: only available here]**: we immerse impressionable minds, from preschool through 8th grade, in a seamlessly **[benefit #2: pain free]** bilingual school experience, French and English together.

One day you're solving math problems in French. The next day you're exploring the wonders of science in English. Back and forth (though more French than English; that's the immersion part).

Our goal: when students leave here, they are fully fluent in two languages and many cultures **[benefit #3: enrichment]**. And their intellects are bigger, not just metaphorically ... but in fact **[benefit #4: better brain development]**. Neuroscience reports there are lifelong cognitive advantages for children who receive an early bilingual education.

Welcome to the French-American School of Rhode Island.

Most people have never experienced a school quite like this **[benefit #5: exclusive advantages for your child]**. We recruit wonderful, innovative, patient, expert teachers **[benefit #6: great staff]**. The special kind of teacher able to bring a shy, tentative child into bloom **[benefit #7: an unpromising child can succeed here]** in both English and French.

By the way, the legendary rigor of the French curriculum is not a myth. We help children become emancipated, responsible, good citizens as well as successful students **[benefit #8: it's more than just an education, it's a life]**.

For families who want to give their child a great start in

life **[benefit #9: parents can congratulate themselves for making the right choice]**, and value diversity and a wider worldview **[benefit #10: ditto]**, there's nothing like the French-American School of Rhode Island.

Most of the time, in my opinion, nonprofits tell the wrong stories. The things insiders often care about most – the nuts and bolts of how things get done – are the things donors usually care about least. Donors are in it for the emotional kick.

"That good feeling you get by writing a check to your favorite charity could be your brain patting itself on the back," the Chicago Tribune wrote recently. "Reporting in Friday's issue of the journal Science, a team of economists and psychologists at the University of Oregon have found that donating money to charity activates regions of the brain associated with pleasure."

You're pushing emotional pleasure. Keep that in mind as you write your case.

■ On the issue of loss

People hate to lose stuff they value. And I'm not speaking rhetorically. I'm reporting a discovery – an important discovery for fundraisers – made by psychologist, Dr. Robert Cialdini.

He tested which motivator would prove more powerful, loss or gain. He observed test subjects responding to two pieces of information about the value of saving money.

In one instance, subjects learned how much they would *gain* if they were to save and invest. In the second instance, subjects learned how much they would *lose* if they *didn't* save and invest.

Which do you think triggered more action, the promise of gain or the promise of loss? Conventional wisdom picks gain. But Dr. Cialdini found that the threat of loss moved more – far more – people to act.

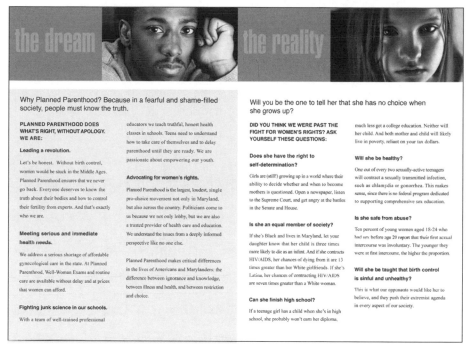

These two pages from the case by Planned Parenthood of Maryland contrast the dream (hope) with the reality (fear and anger).

Fundraisers: tell someone that something they value will be taken away if they don't act – and they are more likely to act. Tell someone in the U.S. that cherished constitutional rights are about to disappear (two examples spring to mind: the right to own firearms and the right to have an abortion upon demand); and they rush to stop the loss.

When the Bush Administration pushed passage of the Patriot Act in the wake of the September 11 attacks, many – liberal and conservative – saw the act as a threat to personal privacy, due process, and maybe even political freedom in the United States. As a result, membership in the American Civil Liberties Union, the ACLU, a network of lawyers and organizers dedicated to defending against such governmental intrusions, doubled in just two years.

13

Day 4:
The Internal Case Emerges

Today you'll be creating your internal case. The internal case is a database of all the messages, arguments and facts which might be useful for raising money for your cause.

The internal case compiles in one document all those bright needles you found yesterday in your research haystack. It also organizes those bright needles for easy reference later.

You could think of your internal case as an exclusive nightclub. You're the gatekeeper behind the velvet rope. And you sharply examine each piece of information, to deem which are suitable for admittance. An internal case eliminates most of the information you've gathered so far; and admits only the best, the brightest, the most compelling, and the most attractive.

■ Your internal case: The mother of all bullet lists

I assemble an internal case in three steps:

• Step one: I enter all the items that I highlighted yesterday into a new document. I make each item a bullet.

• Step two: I annotate each bullet with a few words of boldface type or brief comments. Annotation aids rapid scanning, an ergonomic advantage you'll appreciate when you're trying to find one special item among scores of bullets.

- Step three: I sort my bullets into subcategories.

Internal cases are not meant for public consumption. The writing can be rough, sort of like a "note to self." Here are some bulleted items from actual internal cases, so you can see what these things look like:

- **Every statistic on domestic violence is headed in the wrong direction in VA.** There are more women coming in to seek help with domestic violence every year. There are more families seeking shelter from violence every year. And, most urgently, the number of families TURNED AWAY because the shelter was full jumped 37 percent in the last reported year. *(For a domestic violence shelter in Arlington, VA making the case for expansion; this bullet mentions both urgency and a donor opportunity to end the despair of being turned away.)*

- "Our studies point to the fact that **more and more women are getting infected** through heterosexual relations because their male partners are also [secretly] having sex with men. A large portion of women don't have a clue what their partners' risk factors are." Dr. Helene Gayle, director of the National Center for HIV, STD, and TB-Prevention, reported in NYT. *(For an HIV/AIDS treatment program in DC making the case for expansion; this bullet adds key new information to the story.)*

- In the next 10 years, **persons age 65 and over - those most likely to need hospice care - will increase sharply**. 65+: Anne Arundel county: 54,990 (2000), 61,830 (2010); Prince George's county: 88,350 (2000), 103,050 (2010); TOTAL of both: 143,340 (2000), 164,880

(2010). *(For a hospice in MD making the case for a second facility; this bullet provides the central statistical evidence, that demand for hospice services is about to jump.)*

• **Donors make it happen.** "With your help, we can do amazing things. And without your help, we can't." It's an honest assessment when 75 percent of your income is directly tied to some form of charitable gift, as Audubon RI's is. *(For a conservation and environmental action group making the case for local support; the heavy dependence on donors revealed by the internal case came as news to most of the staff and helped spur a change in attitude, toward increased "donor-centricity.")*

■ Sorting

An internal case remains a disorganized heap until you sort your bullets into subcategories. Sorting finds a place for everything. Over the years I've tried many schemes for sorting. But I've found I need just five subcategories (and thanks to Ron Arena for introducing me to the first three):

• **"Why us?"** What are you doing that's so uniquely wonderful that the world should want more of it and support your mission and vision?

• **"Why now?"** What's the big hurry? What changed? Why is this crucial now? Why can't it wait?

• **"Why you, the donor, might care?"** Why are donors critical to your vision? Have you made them the heroes? What are your emotional triggers? What is the philanthropic opportunity you have to offer? What part of the world will the donor save or change through you?

• The fourth subcategory is for your **organization's history** and information about how programs work. I call this "reassurance" information: donors don't care about it all that much, but they will occasionally have questions.

• The fifth subcategory is a dumping ground **for bright ideas**. When you compile an internal case, you are still in brainstorming mode. Don't prejudge any bright ideas that come to mind. Great ideas sometimes sound ridiculous at first, because they're truly new and different. Hold onto them; see if they evolve. You can always discard them later.

Let's look at the kinds of items that end up under each of these five subcategories. I've selected a representative handful from the 60 or so items that made up the internal case for the Rhode Island Free Clinic's expansion plans.

You'll notice one thing right away: these bullets are roughly cut; they are not polished gems. Remember, an internal case is a source document for staff and board use. It's an idea bank. Prospects do not see it.

These are actual bullets from the clinic's actual internal case.

"Why us?"

• At the Free Clinic, patients with no health insurance get the best health care available in America. What will you see here? Not what health care is in the United States. But what it *could* be, if insurance companies were removed from the picture. **The Rhode Island Free Clinic is how all health care should work.**

• **"Why now?"**

We have the doctors; they're lined up waiting to get in. These are often medical residents. They are learning a lifetime of compassion here. They want to take part in medicine as people wish it could be practiced. **What we don't have is the space or the equipment for extra examining rooms.**

Impact of Your Major Gift to NCLR

NCLR's legal programs and services are always free to everyone. But the legal system is costly. Here are some examples of what your major gift will make possible:

$150,000   will help to win protection for non-biological parents in Texas. This amount would cover half of the costs of one precedent-setting impact court case.

$100,000   will enable NCLR to train legal aid attorneys in Colorado, New Mexico, and Wisconsin who are unfamiliar with LGBT law and its nuances.

$50,000   will cover the cost of creating and distributing a free DVD and resource CD about LGBT foster youth to service providers, legal advocates, and youth across the country.

$25,000   will cover the cost of one week of mediating an anti-discrimination case on behalf of a same-sex couple wishing to live together, as a couple, in a mainstream retirement community.

$15,000   will cover the cost of one expert psychologist testifying on behalf of a recently out lesbian community college coach in court for one week.

$10,000   will send NCLR attorneys to Oklahoma, Texas, North Carolina, Utah, and Florida to give free legal workshops to members of the LGBT community in those states.

$5,000   will cover the cost of providing attorney assistance for twenty callers on our free legal helpline.

$2,500   will cover the cost of distributing *Lifelines*, NCLR's publication on legally protecting your relationship, free of cost to 1,000 people across the country.

$1,500   will send an NCLR attorney to a national conference on immigration to speak to other lawyers about how they can better protect and advocate for the LGBT immigrant community.

National Center for Lesbian Rights
2007 Giving Campaign
870 Market Street Suite 370
San Francisco CA 94102
phone 415.392.6257 x303
fax 415.392.8442
dzalduahilkene@nclrights.org
www.nclrights.org/donate

NATIONAL CENTER FOR LESBIAN RIGHTS

This page in its 2007 case for major donors perfectly answers "Why you, the donor, are so important." NCLR emphasizes two key points: (1) its precedent-

• **"Why you, the donor, are so important?"**

In a just world, no one should die from treatable disease just because they're poor and have no health insurance. **Anecdote heard in an interview shows the problem:** Guy called. Mid 50s. Almost in tears. Laid off 2 years before. Had a heart attack. Still looking for work. His wife works. No health insurance though. After the rent gets paid, the couple has $200 per month left over for everything else they need. Now he's having all the signs again of a heart attack. But he is afraid to tell his wife. He's afraid to go to the emergency room because of the bills. He's calling RIFC while his wife is at work, so she doesn't know.

• Your gifts allow us to expand in two directions: time and space. If we had more examining rooms, we could trim our waiting list by allowing more MDs to rotate through. We could also expand our schedule and cover more days of the week.

History

• What is the **history of the Free Clinic Movement**? Answer: Born out of the radical sixties, free clinics have developed as primary care clinics in response to the plight of the uninsured. Hundreds of free clinics have developed often independent and local solutions.

Bright ideas

• **Maybe a headline:** *"If the clinic's free, how good could it be? Hint: What comes after good, better ...?"*

setting services are free to anyone who seeks justice, yet (2) the work is costly. The superbly skimmable list that follows takes the prospective donor on a quick imaginative journey, exploring the exciting potential for change represented by major gifts at different levels. Design: Orange Square.

■ Bottom line: One band, one sound

Your internal case gathers all your best messages in one place. And that's important to your success as a fundraising operation.

Direct mail, speeches, proposals, newsletters, annual reports, brochures, news releases, the website – in a well-coordinated fundraising program, all sing the same tune.

They reinforce each other. Use the same talking points. Have the same good answers to the three "why" questions. Share the same vision, theme, and goal. Speak in the same clear, concise, consistent voice. "One band, one sound," as Dr. Lee insists to his students in *Drumline*, an inspiring movie about championship college marching bands. Every mouth delivering a different message is cacophony. It's just noise. Many mouths singing the same message is an uplifting choir.

14

Day 5: Start Writing

(But how long should a case be?)

You've finished your research. You've compiled your internal case. Now you're ready to write something that will eventually land in front of prospects' eyes.

And you might be wondering, "How long does it have to be? What's the right length for a case?" A wise professional will automatically answer, "As long as it needs to be, to tell your story effectively." True enough. Not much of a guideline, though.

Here's what I've learned: cases don't have to be long. The average length of a case I write is about 2,200 words, which is the length of a midsized article in a magazine. Some actual word counts:

WORD COUNT	CASE FOR...
936	A regional family services agency with an annual budget under $500,000
975	A big-city symphony seeking three years of bridge funding
1,189	An expanding domestic violence shelter
1,527	A $25 million campaign for a new hospital emergency department

WORD COUNT	CASE FOR...
1,540	General support, for a private bilingual immersion school, K-8
1,600	A child and family service agency with a $3 million annual budget
1,601	A national community service agency with a presence on hundreds of college campuses
1,657	A surgical research institute at a children's hospital
1,682	A tutoring program serving thousands of inner-city public school kids
1,926	An urban Montessori school
2,096	A new HIV/AIDS clinic
2,222	A symphony establishing a $10 million endowment
2,399	A university founding an arts institute
2,775	General support, for a leading college of theology
3,405	A nonprofit builder of affordable housing
4,125	20 new endowed chairs at a university, at $2 million apiece. Each chair had its own description, which together consumed about 85 percent of the text.
4,636	General support, for a national faith-based nonprofit operating homes for people with disabilities

15

What Do We Call It?

Choosing a theme for your campaign

Nothing is likely to receive as much anguished attention from the campaign committee as choosing a theme. Don't torture yourself. Honestly, almost any reasonable name will do.

Your theme is a banner. You march under it toward a special goal. But does it matter what the banner says? Not much.

Your theme simply distinguishes "the campaign" from your other, more routine fundraising activities.

Here are some samples from campaigns I've worked on:

• The New Zoo: The Campaign to Make Roger Williams Park Zoo Exceptionally Great — Again

• Urgent: The Campaign for a New St. Luke's *(for a new emergency department)*

• It's Live! The Campaign for Great Music Forever *(for a symphony endowment)*

• Endowed Chairs at Colgate University: Academic Leadership in the 21st Century

• The Emergence of Stony Brook

• The Campaign for the Next Century *(for a historic home in need of repairs)*

THE MOMENT

OUR MOVEMENT

YOUR NCLR

NATIONAL CENTER FOR LESBIAN RIGHTS

This is the cover for NCLR's 2007 giving campaign. The theme: *We have arrived at the tipping point.* The text of the brochure begins, "Today, true comprehensive legal equality is within our reach. Imagine achieving in one year the legal gains that previously took five. Imagine waking up secure in the knowledge that your basic rights and intimate relationships are protected. After decades of effort, we have arrived at the tipping point, and there is abundant reason for hope..." Design: Orange Square.

• Sanctuary Plus: The Campaign to Expand My Sister's Place *(for a women's shelter)*

• The Be Exceptional Campaign *(for a private school)*

• Prelude: Step One of a Three-Step Campaign *(for a symphony's campaign to cover a structural deficit)*

• The Campaign to Do More *(for a women's shelter)*

Capital Quest, a U.S. consulting firm, has this advice: "[A campaign theme is] usually three to five words that summarize the VISION of the campaign, focusing on the benefits to the community of a successful campaign."

An online search will quickly turn up dozens of ideas for potential themes. A search under the keywords "university capital campaign," for example, quickly produced dozens of options including:

• **The straightforward** (Campaign for Purdue)

• **The anniversary related** (Centennial Campaign)

• **The forward looking** (Campaign for Delaware: Positioning the College for the Future)

• **The majestic** (A Grand Destiny: The Penn State Campaign)

• **Those suggesting "giving back"** ("Generations" Campaign at Notre Dame)

• **Strong emotions** (The Miami University Campaign: For Love and Honor)

• **The pursuit of excellence** (A New Vision of Excellence: The Campaign for Central Michigan University)

Here's what you do.

At that scary, indecisive moment, when your name-picking committee comes down to just a handful of top contenders, there's just one relevant question you need to ask, "Which name will raise more money?"

If none seems to have an advantage, put them all in a hat.

Now pick one.

16

The Marketing Brief: Your Skeleton

In the internal case you answered the three big questions:

• Why is our organization uniquely effective at delivering results?
• Why are gifts so urgent?
• How can we show that the mission's/vision's success depends on philanthropic support?

You have your answers. Now, write up a summary of those answers in 200-300 words. That summary is what we call a "marketing brief."

Write it any way you want. Don't worry about getting it tight and tidy. The marketing brief is for your benefit; it is not for publication. The brief is an important preliminary step, before you dive into writing the case itself. The brief is a map, showing you where your story is headed and how the different parts of your story connect.

"Keep in mind," says fundraising superstar, Mal Warwick, "that the marketing [brief] is ... simply a way to get started." It is a skeleton, the structure beneath the surface, he points out. The case you write will "put flesh on those bones."

Here's an example of an actual marketing brief, written for a research university trying to whip up alumni support:

> It can easily take a century and more (Harvard wasn't always Harvard, after all) to reach the world-renowned level that [we here at Underfunded U.] have already achieved in faculty, scientific specialties, life-changing research, economics, and medicine. And we've only been at it for a few decades. But there is one thing we *are* deficient in, compared to our peer universities (and that would be great research campuses like MIT, Stanford, Columbia, Berkeley): donations and donors. [Underfunded U.] needs your support. Donors make an essential difference. How far do we have to go to catch up? The exalted University of Michigan at Ann Arbor, our academic peer in world-class research, raises $175 million each and every year from donors to its general fund. [Underfunded U.] raises a tenth of that, in its best year. And the lack of donor investment is starting to pinch. [Underfunded U.] needs much larger reserves of scholarship money and endowment to compete for the best students and maintain its first-tier status. The state provides no more than 20% of our annual budget. We can't take the next step (or even stay even) without you, the donor.

The marketing brief frames the tale.

It suggests the kinds of emotional hot buttons the fully-realized case will try to push: (1) the hope that Underfunded U. will compete successfully with its academic peers, if it *does* attract sufficient donor support; and (2) the fear that its first-tier status is threatened, if it *doesn't* attract sufficient donor support.

The brief lays out a common sense argument. "Look, we're competing in the same talent market as far richer universities. Our relative poverty (philanthropically speaking) places us at real disadvantage. Donors make the difference."

Those two things are all that an effective case really needs: emotional hooks and a decently argued rationale. The rest is filler and supporting evidence.

The purpose of the brief is for stakeholders to reach agreement on what the case will contain. The marketing brief is meant for internal use only, so it is not particularly word-smithed. The brief is not the place to hold back.

■ One more for the road: The marketing brief for a Children's Sciences Institute

This case will convince prospective donors that creation of the Children's Sciences Institute (CSI) will lead directly to revolutionary advances in the world of pediatric surgery. These advances will have profound impact both locally, benefiting children in our region who come to us for healing; and globally, as these advances are adopted in other surgical theaters worldwide.

CSI requires $17 million of donor commitment. This philanthropic investment will bring into existence a striking new asset for [big city] Children's Hospital, already highly regarded nationally. When funded, CSI will add to the hospital within just 18 months a made-to-lead research facility devoted exclusively to pushing the envelope of pediatric surgery.

From CSI's research will come impressive new treatments in major areas of children's surgical care. These treatments will improve survival rates and equip pediatric surgeons with more effective, more sophisticated, less invasive techniques. The plan calls for work in four specialties initially: trauma (the number one reason for children's admissions to hospitals); cancer; fetal repair; and pediatric gastroenterology including intestinal reconstruction.

Dr. [X], one of America's top pediatric surgeons and a widely published researcher, will direct CSI. [Big city] recruited Dr. [X] in 2007 from the [other] Hospital Medical Center, one of the nation's top institutions.

The concept for CSI is something Dr. [X] has refined for years. CSI will recruit some of the world's rarest creatures: top pediatric surgeons with huge, proven potential for research breakthroughs – and give them the laboratories, the support, and the funding to achieve miracles; as well as a new home here in [big city], on the hospital's surgical staff.

The $17 million is a first-stage goal. CSI has on the drawing board a second, expanded stage. Exceeding the goal means CSI can move further, faster.

17

Writing Ills?
The Doctor Is In

A case is nothing like a grant proposal, for one good reason: the reader.

The reader of a grant proposal is paid to read every bloody, arduous, tortured sentence you write. The reader of a case is not. Cases are read by volunteers, granting you a few minutes of their precious time. At the end of which, they might make a gift of their hard-earned cash.

I repeat: your target audience in a case is comprised of volunteers who might decide to give you money. Confuse them, frustrate them, bore them, exhaust them at your peril.

■ Make it a conversation

Brigitte Mertling says of her case writing: "I think of it as a conversation in the recipient's head. I use the word 'you' a lot. It is not in the Queen's English. It's more accessible and more comfortable."

George Smith, dean of UK direct mail writers, agrees. "All fundraising copy should sound like someone talking," he comments in his guide, *Tiny Essentials of Writing for Fundraising*.

Does the following phrasing sound to you like conversation?

"The university's strategic plan ... identifies strategies to enhance the university's work for students on three fronts...."

This snippet is real, by the way. It's from a brand-name university's first attempt at a case. But honestly, have you ever in normal conversation said anything remotely like the phrase, "identify strategies"? Told a friend, for instance: "I have the place to myself all weekend, so I've identified strategies that will enhance how I spend my time."

Jacked-up business and academic clichés like "identify strategies" add nothing to your case. People see through them and distrust them. These phraseologies slap a coat of lazy pretension over otherwise simple thoughts. Here's the same idea said conversationally (and with donor-centric emphasis): "The new plan hopes, with your help, to improve the university in three ways...."

That was easy, right?

■ Don't do the dance of the four veils

For the most part, nonprofit communications are boring. Not on purpose, mind you. Still, they are almost always uninteresting, my vast exposure to them suggests. And why? Because they swaddle themselves in one or more of the following interest-draining veils.

VEIL #1: They reject any mention of conflict.

Ditto: controversy. Ditto: uncomfortable truths. Ditto: "anything that might upset people."

Conflict and controversy are the essence of drama. Drama automatically engages and intrigues readers, because our brains are wired to respond to such stimuli. Drama moves people. Drama overcomes indifference and inertia. And indifference and inertia are your real enemies when you're trying to communicate, particularly when you're trying to fundraise.

An absence of drama leaves readers bored, cold, unmoved, indifferent.

Does your mission *naturally* lack drama? Doubtful. Many, maybe most, charitable missions are in some way a solution to a serious problem: teenagers in trouble, disappearing natural habitat, disease, ignorance, chronic poverty. Problems like these are inherently dramatic.

Bear in mind, too, that the problems you're attempting to solve are exactly what makes your agency seem relevant to donors, prospects, the media and others. If you climb aboard "the Happy Talk Express" and avoid drama at all costs, your communications ring false and your organization seems less relevant.

VEIL #2: A tendency to prefer weak, bland words to bold, vivid words.

Consider headline verbs, for example.

Here's a collection of verbs plucked from headlines in *The Wall Street Journal*: *mauled, devour, looms, spark, threaten, embrace, sputters, sowing, surge, reject, retools, blames, loses, clash, expand.* What characterizes this collection of verbs? Vigor, sound, fury, sharp action. In sum: these verbs have impact.

Newspaper editors have a saying: The verb *is* the story. *Surges?* The trend is up. *Collapses?* The trend is down. Verbs are fireworks, motion, attitude.

Here's a collection of verbs, though, that I scoured from headlines in nonprofit newsletters: *establishes, listed, use, unite, reach, give back, plan, unifies, build, sets, visits, shares, administer, awards, help, benefits.*

What characterizes *this* collection of verbs? They are inconclusive (*shares*), weak (*administer*), loftier than need be (*unifies*), and flat (*visits*, as in *visits an issue*). In sum: no impact.

VEIL #3: Faint (if any) appreciation for the emotional basis behind all human response.

Instead of fear, anger, hope, and salvation, we are served extra helpings of pontification.

As noted earlier, with modern MRI diagnostics, we can now watch the brain fire as it makes a decision. It fires first in the emotional seat, then the impulse routes through the rational seat. Imagine the rational part of your brain as a flunky armed with a rubber stamp that says, in formidable letters, APPROVED. The emotions decide what to do. The rational part of your brain seconds the decision: *Approved*.

The old thinking held that emotions and reasoning were opposites. They struggled for dominance. The well-informed thinking now knows that emotions initiate the decision, and the reasoning area of your brain struggles to keep up with a "Yes, dear."

VEIL #4: JARGON.

Allowing jargon into your case is a faux pas. It's a mildly disgusting habit, something you don't do in front of guests, like flossing at the dinner table.

Here's a United Way of my acquaintance explaining itself: "Our awareness and efforts now focus on community impact goals, and how we feed into that. *In other words*," [my emphasis added], "our work has become driven more by mission than by function. We need the multi-pronged approach to move public will, and there has been an exponential benefit of working more closely and in concert."

In other words? This writer needs help. *Real* "other words" would have said something obvious like, "We've changed the way we do things. We hope to get better results this way. Our first attempt was a big success."

Jargon is not public language. It's for specialists only. Words like "interdisciplinary," that bring to mind all sorts of positive connotations among educators, do not resonate the same way for the average person.

And the average person — not a specialist – is your target audience. When the University of Toronto raised a billion dollars recently, 112,819 people made gifts. It's safe to assume that very few were specialists conversant with academic jargon.

Return to the example of non-conversational writing that opened this chapter. The full text reads as follows:

> XYZ University's strategic plan is designed to amplify the university's academic excellence. The result of a 13-month planning effort, the plan identifies strategies to enhance the university's work for students on three fronts:
>
> • Reinterpreting the liberal arts skills of communication and critical thinking to take into account 21st-century challenges and opportunities
>
> • Multiplying connections between students and faculty members by building on the faculty's record of original research and creativity
>
> • Building on XYZ University's strong sense of community, locally and globally

What's wrong with this sort of writing? At least three things: (1) it's freighted with jargon, the kind of bureaucrat-ese only insiders understand; (2) it mentions no emotional goals; and (3) the donor is nowhere in sight. Here's a rewrite that covers the very same ground, but eliminates all the flaws:

> Within a decade, if all goes according to plan, XYZ University will emerge as the top school in its class, leaving behind our 'peer schools' of today. Admittedly, the plan is ambitious. And it won't be cheap: excellence in education at this level never

is. But we will get there, thanks to your vision, your commitment, and your help.

There's no jargon. The donor is given all the credit in the last sentence. And what are the "emotional goals"? (I.e., goals that touch the heart of the target audience.) There are several: emerging as the top school in its class, leaving behind its peer schools, and pursuing an ambitious (as opposed to ordinary) plan. These are all things the alumni understand, appreciate, and want. How do I know? I've asked.

Final word goes to the brothers Heath, from their business bestseller, *Made to Stick*: "Concrete language helps people, especially novices, understand new concepts. Abstraction is the luxury of the expert." What does "concrete" mean? "If you can examine something with your senses, it's concrete. A V8 engine is concrete. 'High-performance' is abstract. Most of the time, concreteness boils down to specific people doing specific things."

18

Telling Your Story (1)

Going from A to B

"Every communication has as its goal to take the audience from where they are at the start of your presentation, which is *Point A*, and move them to your objective, which is *Point B*," Jerry Weissman says in his sumptuously useful book *Presenting to Win: The Art of Telling Your Story*. "This dynamic shift is persuasion."

At the beginning of a presentation, Mr. Weissman notes, the typical audience is uninformed, dubious, and resistant. By the end of a great presentation, they understand the idea, believe in the idea, and are ready to act in support of the idea.

He's talking about convincing wary investors to buy stock in a new public company. But he might as well be talking about fundraising. Virtually all prospective donors will be, to some degree, uninformed, dubious, and resistant. Your case seeks to change all that.

And treating donors as investors is not a metaphorical gesture. They *are* your investors: they put money into your mission and vision so that you can make something good happen in the world.

"Keep in mind, always, that people give in order to get. They don't simply want to give away their money; they want to feel they're investing it and getting something in return," writes David Lansdowne, author of *The Relentlessly Practical Guide to Raising Serious Money*. "To succeed, you must explain exactly why you seek the funding, why your project is compelling, who will benefit, and why the money is needed now. In other words, your needs – presented as opportunities – must be specific, people-oriented, and have a sense of urgency."

■ Putting Weissman and Lansdowne to work: An example

Let's pretend.

We're writing a case for a U.S. research institute with a promising new initiative in the works: a possible cure for Alzheimer's.

Today's goal is to write a 100-word executive summary. It's not a lot of words. But there is a huge amount at stake. After all, the executive summary is the first real text the reader encounters in the document. And it distills and sets up the rest of the case. The summary needs to be rational, emotional, determined, and compelling: all within 100 words.

We grab a pen. Take a deep breath. Within easy reach, for moral support, rest the books by Weissman and Lansdowne.

First we write our A.

Point A explains where we are now on this grave issue. It spotlights two colliding facts, about life spans and disease:

> People live longer in America all the time. And for 3 out of 5, it's a very bitter ending ... for themselves and their families. Why? Because today 3 out of 5 Americans over the age of 85 get Alzheimer's. That's a fact.[1]

---

[1] Feel free to steal this example if it helps you. But do check my made-up facts. I have no idea what percentage of U.S. citizens over age 85 get Alzheimer's.

Not too shabby. We've summed up a national health crisis in a mere 43 words.

Now let's write our B. Point B is where we want to go, where this project will take us. It's our *objective*, to use Weissman's term. Point B should also fulfill Lansdowne's criteria; and be specific, people-oriented, and urgent. We start by making a promise:

> But this grim outlook could soon improve.
>
> Our unique research could help shrink the number afflicted with Alzheimer's significantly, maybe down to 1 in 5 – within a decade.
>
> We're ready. Our research to date has been called the most promising approach ever found. But we need your help. The crucial next stage depends almost entirely on donor support.

Done. Grand total: 103 words that together frame the rest of the document. Cover to cover, the entire case might stretch to 3,000 words of supporting evidence and plans. But in the first hundred or so, the reader has discovered exactly what the project intends to accomplish and what a philanthropic investment could achieve.

■ What the rest of the case consists of

The campaign veterans at Compton, in their enlightening book *Capital Fundraising in the UK - The Compton Way*, offer a checklist of things that a case should touch on. The case statement must concisely tell a story which explains your:

- Reason for being
- History
- Achievements
- Challenges
- Response

- Project benefits
- Cost breakdown
- Proposed fundraising methodology
- Pace-setting leadership
- Recognition opportunities (recognition of how much donors matter, in my opinion; for many campaigns, the donor is essential, because without charitable contributions, no vision will be realized, no goal attained)
- Tax-effectiveness (this is a footnote at best; surveys show that the tax-deductibility of U.S. contributions has little bearing on giving except among the filthy rich ... maybe)
- Vision for the future

Compton assumes that you're doing your due diligence and conducting a resources (i.e., feasibility) study before you try to raise millions of dollars. That's why the checklist includes early-stage essentials like "pace-setting leadership." The term refers to that portion of your case where you reveal exactly who has pledged substantial gifts to launch your campaign, those precious so-called "lead gifts."

19

Telling Your Story (2)

Deconstructing an actual case

Let's look at the structure of an actual case written a few years ago by a major consulting firm for a $30 million campaign. The client was a U.S. fraternal organization that operates retirement communities.

The case has eight sections, totaling 4,554 words and required nine interviews.

Section 1: The welcome message. It's brief, just 72 words long. It explains the campaign theme, which focuses on "home." On the same page is a photo of one of the organization's retirement homes.

Section 2: The introduction. Again, it's not long: just six paragraphs totaling 288 words. The introduction thanks readers for taking a few moments. It touches again on the meaning of home. And it specifies the need: $30 million for "a number of significant capital projects," improvements to existing homes. At the top of the page is a poem about this organization's tradition of generosity. The introduction ends with the phrase: "...first, let's step back in time," neatly transitioning to the next section.

Section 3: The organization's history. This stretches to 10 paragraphs totaling 500 words. It sets the context for the campaign and reveals a century-long track record of caring. It opens with an inspirational quote and closes with a quote about generosity. There is a 250-word sidebar on the page that explains the fraternal organization to prospects who aren't members.

Section 4: The organization's philosophy. The philosophy emphasizes "care...and caring." In just 144 words, the case explains the organization's concept behind a wonderful nursing/retirement home. There is a photo of a happy couple who reside there and a caption that begins "Meet some residents." The section closes with a quote from a doctor, commenting approvingly on the care provided at these homes.

Section 5: Why our mission matters today. This section brings

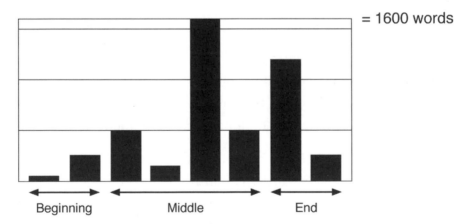

= 1600 words

Beginning Middle End

This chart shows the relative lengths of the 8 sections in the case. Note how brief the beginning sections are. That's good. The reader isn't warmed up, so you start with easy, quick stuff. The middle section is where you dump in the kitchen sink: plans, history. And the end is the ask and the thank you. This "narrative profile" — a quick, easy beginning; a satisfying ending; and a long middle full of explanation — is exactly the same formula taught in film school and followed by most Hollywood films.

the reader up to date on the organization's scope of service. But it never wanders far from the campaign: the section opens with a quote from the CEO about why $30 million is urgently important now. At 1,600 words this is the longest section, but much of it is background. Descriptions of current facilities account for its extended length. There are five testimonials from residents and board members scattered around and breaking up the text. There is a quote from the director of the Alzheimer's unit. Visual relief is minimal. There is an interior photo of a dining room and an exterior photo of a stately facility.

Section 6: The vision. A quote from the chair opens this section. He talks briefly about the vision. A 500-word article follows summarizing what the organization has added to its facilities in the past three years and what *will* be added once this campaign is finished. There's another "Meet the resident" photo. The section closes with a quote from the CEO about the region's dire need for quality nursing homes.

Section 7: The call to action. This section opens with a quote from the foundation chairman calling for gifts. It devotes 1,200 words to what will be built with the $30 million. And it ends with a bullet list summarizing those same items.

Section 8: A closing thank you. This 250-word wrap up opens with a quote from the foundation president stressing this fraternal organization's proud legacy of caring. It pleads, "Won't you give?" It includes yet another "Meet the resident" photo. And it ends with an uplifting quote about doing good.

20

Telling Your Story (3)

Treat your donor as the solution

The Shasta Community Health Center didn't dance around the issue. It labeled the opening section of its case statement, "Challenge." And the very first sentence delivered a deluge of bad news:

"Without building a new health center, Shasta County's primary source of health care for the working poor and indigent, Shasta Community Health Center, will close." The deadline for shutting down: June 2001.

But that didn't happen. Today Shasta Community Health Center thrives. It pursues its special mission ("...providing preventive, acute and chronic health care services to the economically or otherwise disadvantaged") at five attractive locations.

Shasta ultimately raised $4.5 million in that desperate first capital campaign, guided by Capital Quest consultants. Who deserves the real credit, though? The consultants? A bit. The Shasta health professionals? Absolutely; because they had a credible story to tell. But in the end the true heroes are the donors. They solved this particular problem by investing in the project. Without the donors, success wasn't possible. With the donors, it was.

Treating your donors as the crucial solution to an important problem will do your fundraising a world of good. When you take that approach (it's called "donor-centricity," a topic we return to in a later chapter), you shift responsibility – and the credit – for achieving the vision *off* your shoulders and *onto* the donors' shoulders, where it properly belongs.

Donors want that responsibility – and they deserve the credit that ensues as well, once lives are saved, the world has changed, and the vision expressed in the case is realized.

Do not write your story as if donors are merely kind, generous bystanders. They are *not* bystanders. You cannot achieve what you set out to achieve *without* gobs of donor support. Make that point brilliantly clear. Write the donor into your story, as the essential solution.

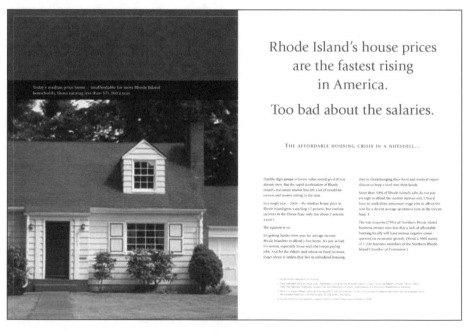

Before the donor can become a solution, you have to have a problem. A nonprofit builder of affordable housing opens its case by clearly defining the problem.

■ Are you inviting your donors to a fight?

In 2008, *The New York Times* reported on a theory proposed by Yale economics professor, Dean Karlan, regarding why small donors contribute money to political campaigns.

He said, "Giving is not a calculation of what you are buying." Big donors buy access and influence. But a $25 gift to Barack Obama's presidential campaign is not about that, Dr. Karlan concluded. "It is about participating in a fight."

I firmly believe, based on my own charitable giving and the feelings I have when I write those checks or make those gifts online, that Dr. Karlan has hit the emotional nail on the head.

Many gifts originate with a desire to mix it up, to get into a fight that we think matters, and to win. The fight to beat childhood cancer, the fight to clean up city government, the fight to end abuse of elders in nursing homes, the fight to bring polluters to justice ... the list is endless.

Talking about winning a fight is yet another way to position donors as the solution.

21

Telling Your Story (4)

The AIDA Formula

In a case for support, *telling* your story is *selling* your story.

There's an ancient "story-selling" formula that can help. It's called the AIDA formula and it reliably moves a prospect from ignorance to action..

AIDA is an acronym for a four-step journey, *Attention Interest Desire Action*. Sales trainers around the world teach AIDA. Advertising agencies around the world use it to market products and services. The sequence unfolds like this:

1) You grab the prospect's ATTENTION somehow. (At the start, the audience is indifferent and inert. Your job is to make them alert. This is why advertising works so hard to call attention to itself.)

2) You say something to your target audience that builds INTEREST.

3) You make a promise or an offer that's crafted to stimulate DESIRE in your specific target audience.

4) You issue an urgent call to ACTION.

I've used the AIDA formula many times to make a case. Here, for instance, are three sample openers, the A's in AIDA:

• Every year more than 3,000 Providence public school students face some kind of learning crisis that could end their chances of a successful school career. And then one of our volunteer tutors walks in the door.

• It's way too easy for a kid around here to get into trouble. Pregnancy. Drugs. Crime. Dropping out. Do you ever wonder how those kids get out of trouble and find a future again?

• For an agency made necessary by drug and alcohol abuse, teen pregnancy, child depression, youth unemployment, truancy and dropping out, family violence, runaways, homelessness, and petty crime … we're remarkably happy. Must be all the changes we see in the people we help.

Or consider the front covers (*see next two pages*) of the case brochures for a zoo and a domestic violence shelter. These are examples of A's.

Grabbing someone's attention is the easy part. Tell me something I didn't know, show me an uncommon photo, bring me into a scene, surprise me in any fashion – and I'll pay attention momentarily. To keep me interested, though, you need to mention something I care about. A's simply get me to pay attention. I's keep me reading and get me on the road toward desire.

From actual cases, here are some I's in the AIDA sequence:

• A symphony is a tough business. Every time you perform, you lose money … if you depend on ticket sales alone. *(Since the target audience for this case will be lovers of live classical music, it's safe to assume they will be interested in the things that threaten a symphony's existence.)*

• Today at St. Luke's Hospital. The emergency room is crowded.

What are the attention-getting details of these case covers? A teasing question for a zoo, with a giraffe photo that doesn't, for once, feature a neck. For

security reasons, a women's shelter can't reveal itself; instead, construction of a new facility becomes an anonymous board with a note nailed to it.

Your wait is long. The demand for surgery is growing. And there are not enough beds. *(Since the target audience for this community hospital are people living within its service area, it's safe to assume they will want to improve conditions in an emergency room where they and their loved ones might end up.)*

• French education has a certain reputation. Academically demanding. A no-nonsense approach. With all the tough talk, you might not guess our secret ingredients: love and respect. *(Since the target audience is parents of students at a private bilingual school, it's safe to assume they will respond to revelations about the school's surprising warmth. It doesn't hurt, either, that there are great photos of kids throughout the case.)*

Material that might prove interesting to prospects often makes up the bulk of a case. This material includes all the supporting information: your organization's history, your accomplishments, brief descriptions of your programs, answers to the prospects' most frequently asked questions, and such.

Desire – the D in AIDA – is easy. For one thing, you never make a case to someone who isn't somehow predisposed to make a gift. When you solicit those 100-150 top prospects, you have good reason through your research to approach certain people. They weren't picked at random. They have some potential personal reason for caring: e.g., they're music lovers, they live in a hospital's service area, they have kids in your school.

Desire for some promised result is what moves a prospect to become a donor. The donor's desire is *fulfilled* when all the gifts are in and the vision comes to life. The two final letters of AIDA – desire and urgent action – are commonly linked in cases. Here are some examples:

• Is dual-language really "the best education money can buy?" Many think so. But tuition alone won't buy everything this school needs. Our future depends on your generosity.

• The Rhode Island Philharmonic vision: A great orchestra and a great music school, together delivering outstanding service to the community ... with a safe, sustainable financial future, thanks to a large and permanent endowment. We'll take care of the first part. The rest is up to you.

• Do you find these facts disturbing? Good. They are. Are you searching for a way to reduce HIV infection here in D.C.? Even better. Time to write a check!

22

Prepare to be Browsed

I review hundreds of fundraising communications in a typical year. And one flaw stands out like Mt. Everest. The vast majority don't cater to the typical reader's habit, which is to browse first before plunging in.

Who knew such a thing mattered? Well, every competent magazine and newspaper editor for starters. Now you do, too.

Here's the unvarnished truth: people do *not* want to read your stuff. Sure, they want to *understand* your stuff and *absorb* your stuff. But spend long stretches of time reading it? Not particularly.

It's partly a symptom of the times we live in; the time-pressed times; the *TMI* times: *Too Much Information* coming at us from every direction.

It's partly because, with all due respect, most fundraising communications are born to be boring; and your case for support is probably no exception.

In our bustling world, if I understand your vision in 15 rather than 30 minutes, that's a good thing. If I understand your vision in five minutes rather than 15, that's even better. And if you could slip me a pill and I'd understand your vision instantly, that would be the best.

Having a good "browser level" delivers the pill form of your case. A well-written browsing level explains your message as quickly as humanly possible and with deep penetrating power.

■ What constitutes the "browser level"?

What's in the browser level? All the items on a page that initially attract the eye.

Studies conducted by German researcher Siegfried Vögele in the 1980s revealed that the human eye predictably flits to graphically distinctive elements before anything else: bigger type, bolder type, briefer type, and pictures. In other words: headlines, subheads, captions, pull quotes, bullet lists, sidebars, photos, charts and other art.

Recent research from the Poynter Institute confirms these tendencies. Photos attracted 75 percent of newspaper readers, headlines 56 percent, and articles just 25 percent or less.

Therein lies the opportunity. Forget about articles; few people read them. Of course, you still have to write articles; just don't drive yourself crazy making them extra-special-super-terrific. Instead, put your best creative energies into your browser level: with explosive headlines, razor-sharp captions, thundering pull quotes, never-seen-before photos, and the like.

■ Your section headlines are your story's structure

If you could *only* tell your story through your browser level – in your headlines, in your captions, and the rest – without any articles at all, what would you choose to say?

When I'm working on a case, I like to write all my headlines first. If I can write clear headlines, then I know that I understand my story. Essentially, the headlines are the outline for the case. It's a bit like

The LGBT community faces a lifetime of challenges.

You can guarantee The HOPE Fund will be here to help, forever.

For a short time, a very special matching fund

In 1994, there were few LGBT-friendly services and fewer agencies able to provide them.

The solution? The HOPE Fund.

In 1994, concerned civic leaders collaborated with the Community Foundation for Southeast Michigan to confront a challenge. The LGBT community desperately

A $2 million endowment will guarantee The HOPE Fund's important work *forever*.

The good news? We're already halfway there!

The HOPE Fund has always welcomed annual gifts, which are immediately used for grants, and gifts to The HOPE Endowment Fund, which are invested for the future.

A very special but time-limited opportunity: the Community Foundation will match your individual or business gift to the endowment.

Your tax-advantaged gift to The HOPE Endowment Fund already means your $1,000 gift only costs $585 or your $10,000 gift only costs $6,435.*

The "forever" of your gift is assured by the Community Foundation for Southeast Michigan.

It's a great partner. The Community Foundation is an independent nonprofit governed by a board of 50 volunteer civic leaders. It is committed to bringing

The right time to give is *now*, before matching dollars run out.

Take advantage of the Community Foundation's generous matching offer before it runs out. You will be investing in the future of our community.

Don't forget your will! Take care of your loved ones and the LGBT community, too.

If you don't have a will or other estate plan in place, Michigan law will write one for you, and the law favors your next of kin rather than individuals or charities of your choice. Ask The HOPE Fund for your free copy of *Estate Planning and Planned Giving for Lesbian, Gay, Bisexual and Transgender Individuals, Couples and their Families*.

Above: The headlines that make up the browser level for a case establishing The HOPE Fund endowment. Note how the argument moves easily and logically from one headline to the next. Written by Rick Schwartz for the Community Foundation for Southeast Michigan; design by Skidmore.

building the skeleton before adding meat to the bones.

Here is an actual set of section headlines from a small case for support:

[section headline #1]

For an agency made necessary by drug and alcohol abuse, teen pregnancy, child depression, youth unemployment, truancy and dropping out, family violence, runaways, homelessness, and petty crime … we're remarkably happy.

Must be all the changes we see in the people we help.

[section headline #2]

What we offer families in the Northwest Corner: Free, convenient counseling when things threaten to get out of control.

[section headline #3]

Housatonic Youth Service Bureau is not just about kids in trouble. It's also about building stronger, more successful kids and families.

[section headline #4]

And you're the hero. So much happens because of your generosity.

[section headline #5]

Now you're invited to change more lives.

Section headline #1 gets quite a lot done in its 43 words. It lays out the history of the place, the scope of the problems the Bureau works on, offers glimpses into the lives of the people it helps, and, most important, reports on success.

Section headline #2 introduces a brief section summarizing who is served and why these services matter.

Section headline #3 introduces a section that briefly describes the Bureau's terrific programs.

Section headline #4 introduces a section which reveals the major role that philanthropy has played in recent years keeping the Bureau open to meet crisis after crisis in the community, despite state budget cuts.

Section headline #5 introduces the vision and overtly invites the donor to act.

When your section headlines by themselves tell your whole story, then you have an effective browser level. And not until.

23

Make Your Case Bigger than You

On May 21, 2007, the last of its kind – the famed tea clipper ship, Cutty Sark – burned at its London dock.

The Cutty Sark, built in 1869 and midway through a major restoration, had been a popular tourist destination. It was the last surviving example of the sail-driven thoroughbreds that once had set the pace for global trade. More than 15 million people had visited the vessel, to absorb the romance of a time and a trade now past.

Commenting on the fire that day, Richard Doughty, chief executive of the Cutty Sark Trust, made his case – and he made it bigger than just a story about a ruined ship.

"I'm relieved," he said. "I came here thinking the ship had gone on her last journey." He tallied the loss, knowing that readers worldwide would hear his plea through countless news reports. "This will have resulted in millions and millions of pounds of damage," Doughty said. "This is a ship that belongs to the world, and we're going to need financial help."

This is a ship that belongs to the world. Now *that's* making a case bigger. *And we're going to need financial help*. With a crystal clear call to action. And financial help arrived: more than ten million

"Democracy has to be born anew every generation, and education is its midwife." ~ John Dewey

Who Needs Campus Compact?

Let's start with America.

Rockford College is one of 39 institutions of higher education that together make up the Illinois Campus Compact. From three member universities in 1985, Campus Compact has expanded into a major national movement, with more than 950 member institutions and 31 state offices.

"We know that connecting studies with problem-solving service in the community deepens, complicates and challenges students' learning. They become citizen scholars who renew our democratic society.... "
~ Toni Murdock, President, Antioch University Seattle

This headline offers a perfect example of making it bigger: we've joined America's fortunes as a democracy directly to the work of an organization fostering community involvement among U.S. college students. Feel free to borrow this idea. The case never made it to print. A change in leadership at Campus Compact took the organization in a different direction.

pounds in charitable contributions. The fully restored Cutty Sark, suspended in air so visitors can pass beneath her to appreciate her speed-enhancing lines, is on schedule to re-open in 2010.

Jerry Panas devotes a long chapter in his wise (and wonderfully entertaining) book, *Making the Case*, to the topic of expanding your vision beyond the boundaries of your project.

The Tampa Museum of Art, for instance, wanted a new facility to show more of its collection and welcome hundreds of thousands of additional visitors. But what did this new facility also mean? It meant busloads of school kids coming to meet important art for the first time. It meant an ordinary portion of riverfront property would be transformed into a magnificent landscape linked to the city's River Walk. It meant a "fatigued downtown" would enjoy some badly needed revitalization, which in turn helped downtown merchants.

"You see where I'm going with this," Jerry writes. "All of a sudden, the program becomes of much greater and multi-magnified consequence than just creating a facility to house more art."

He adds, "You're not just a writer [when you create your case]. You transform dreams into deeds. You search for every felicitous possibility that will make the project more expansive and worthy than the organization itself. Any crack that will open a new door."

24

Put It In a Nutshell, Too

I like to show the campaign's bottom line at a glance. It helps keep readers oriented, I believe.

It can be – and should be – brief. For example:

We Are Exceptional

THE CAMPAIGN FOR SAINT NORMA'S SCHOOL

Three things will make our school exceptional:

Exceptional teachers
Our new Faculty Endowment
Goal: $4 million

Exceptional young people
Our new Student Financial Aid Endowment
Goal: $4 million

Exceptional learning environment
Our new Construction & Renovation Fund
Goal: $13 million

See the next page for related artwork.

The endowment goal: $5 million minimum

"The Rhode Island Philharmonic is at an important crossroads. We've seen enormous improvement as an orchestra. Excellence in every aspect. But that comes at a cost. To sustain this level, we need a permanent endowment."

MARIE LANGLOIS
ENDOWMENT CAMPAIGN CO-CHAIR

A symphony is a tough business. Every time you perform, you lose money … if you depend on ticket sales alone. Consider the National Symphony Orchestra, resident at the Kennedy Center in Washington, DC. The National Symphony earns just 60% of its income from ticket sales. And that's pretty typical. Although in Rhode Island we do a bit better. Here, subscriptions and single-ticket sales earn back 65% of our cost. **Still, it's clearly not enough.**

THE HIGH COST OF CONTINUED EXCELLENCE

NOWHERE AMONG AMERICA'S QUALITY SYMPHONY ORCHESTRAS do ticket prices alone cover the costs of a renowned conductor, top professional musicians, world-class guest artists … not to mention the technical staff, overhead and the rest.

Annual charitable gifts, corporate sponsorships, and the occasional unrestricted bequest make up some of the difference.

But not all. Every year our costs go up, faster than our income. There's always a gap, a so-called "structural deficit." What covers that?

The answer is permanent endowment, a financial safety net that the Rhode Island Philharmonic doesn't yet enjoy.

PERMANENT ENDOWMENT: PRODUCING INCOME FOREVER, IN EVER-INCREASING AMOUNTS

PERMANENT ENDOWMENT IS DIFFERENT. For one thing, the principal can't be invaded. Only the interest income is used.

A portion of that interest helps with annual operating expenses for the Philharmonic and the Music School.

But a portion of the interest is also reinvested in the endowment, guaranteeing that the principal steadily grows and becomes more productive through the decades. (See illustration on page 9.)

Permanent endowment is a remedy hotly pursued by top classical orchestras across the country.

The Boston Symphony Orchestra pockets $6 million a year in income from its endowment. To insure its future, The Philadelphia Orchestra in 2004 launched a $125 million endowment drive, and has raised almost half the goal already.

The point is, every quality orchestra that plans to survive needs a permanent endowment … and one that is as large as possible.

It's the same for the Rhode Island Philharmonic. We need a large permanent endowment to ensure our long-term viability. And we need it soon, because our cash reserves are uncomfortably low.

Or, as Beethoven might score it, not only *grandioso* but *prestissimo*.

Readers want to know your bottom line. If you have a specific dollar goal, proudly announce it.

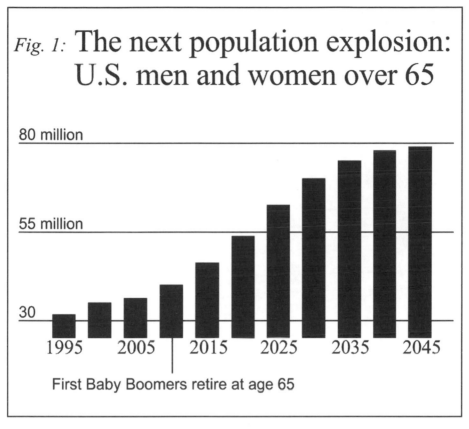

Fig. 1: **The next population explosion: U.S. men and women over 65**

First Baby Boomers retire at age 65

A faith-based provider of assisted living facilities for people over age 65 puts the looming challenge in a nutshell with a graph that demonstrates how big the demand for such housing will become.

25

Take Your Prospect on a Verbal Tour

If only.

If only your prospective donors would take a tour. If only they could see for themselves how impressive your organization's work is ... then your money worries would be over. Personal tours are amazingly persuasive. Prospects with first-hand exposure to your mission tend to fall in love.

There's a problem, though: Who can find time these busy days to schedule a personal tour?

So: consider writing a personal tour into your case.

Invite readers inside your world. Point out telling details. And be sure to *show* as much as *tell*. Ask readers to use their senses: to listen, to smell, to see.

Here's a fragment of a mental tour, excerpted from a draft case for an urban Montessori school. Note the physical details: the color of the paint, the quiet in a busy school, the size of the furnishings. Every detail has meaning.

Come onto the Quantum Montessori "campus" for a

moment.

If your child is in preschool or kindergarten, you're familiar with the old mansion. But you might not know what happens every summer; it's a Quantum sort of thing. Two painters fastidiously apply a fresh coat of the perfect off-white shade to the walls. We repaint the mansion annually, between sessions. "We want it to be impeccably beautiful when the kids return," explains Martin Doe, Head of School.

That's the attention to detail common here.

More indicative, though, is the peculiar sound of a Montessori school when it's full of children in preschool and kindergarten. It's quiet. Everyone remarks on it.

It's not that it's under strict control. It's under *self*-control. Montessori students are doing their work. Except to them it doesn't *seem* like work. It's the work they want to do, the work they've picked themselves. Dr. Montessori believed that children teach themselves if given the appropriate environment and guidance.

That's part of the Montessori secret. Children are happy to be in school because at Montessori "play and work are the same thing," Martin says. That's the Montessori way. E v e n dropping a child at school by car has a "Montessori way." It means being mindful and courteous to other drivers. And teachers shake the hand of each arriving student: "At Montessori it all starts with respect."

Especially respect for the child.

That's why the chairs and desks and sinks and toilets and banisters – and everything else the child interacts with – are scaled to smaller bodies. It is a founding element of the Montessori pedagogy and one of its premier contributions to educational thought: create a small, child-sized microcosm where each child can learn to perform competently.

And there are some fascinating ways children become competent. Having mature responsibilities is one. Children learn to be careful here. They drink from real glass. They pour their drinks from small glass pitchers carried, by the children, on (well, it *is* an old mansion after all) a small silver tray. They polish their own trays to keep them spotless. They tidy up their personal areas. They work well with others. They focus.

■ Ready to write up your tour? Here's how you do it.

You can't give an insightful tour from behind a desk.

Get out of your chair. Make believe you have a friend with you. Walk around with your make-believe friend. And as you two walk, point things out: "See that? Smell that? Hear that? Touch that?" Exercise your senses.

And take notes. Sensory details can reveal a lot.

• "Hear that sound of rushing rubber-soled shoes? Nurses here probably jog ten miles every shift. But you have to be slow as well as fast in medicine. Because you can't make mistakes. That's why we created our nationally recognized quality assurance program..."

• "Smell that sharp odor? That's hot, welded steel. These kids didn't have that odor in their lives until we started this program. And why does it matter? Because it's also the smell of a better future. These kids will have a well-paying job for life, in the steel industry..."

• "Look around. What do you see? Offices, right? But from 4 PM to 8 PM this place transforms. Every door is closed. And behind every door there's a therapist, a troubled kid, and a family desperate for relief. And they get it. It might take months, but we help the family heal, and we bring that kid back."

26

How You Say Things Does Matter

The donor-centric difference

The Several Sources Foundation raises a great deal of money through direct mail. In its highly successful package to acquire new donors, the foundation runs a photo of a swaddled infant with the caption, "Baby Joseph, one of our over 15,000 rescued babies."

Which is one way to say it. But it's not the donor-centric way. Here's a donor-centric rewrite: "Baby Joseph, one of over 15,000 babies rescued by your gifts."

See the difference? The first caption grabs the credit for the organization. The second caption awards all the credit to the donors.

Rewriting a single caption won't do much for your income stream, of course. But adopt a donor-centric voice overall in your fundraising communications, including your case; and you'll see resistance melt.

Benefit #1 to you: you'll raise more money more easily. Benefit #2: you'll retain your donors longer. If you make people feel essential to the successful completion of your mission, they stick around.

Pay attention. Most fundraisers get this wrong.

The "donor-*optional*" way of addressing supporters goes something like this: "We did this. We did that. We were amazing. Oh, by the way, if you happened to be among those who sent in a gift,

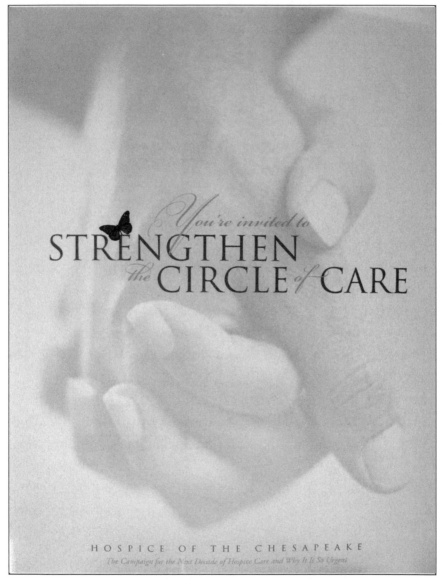

This case invites the prospect to join the campaign right on the cover.

Coming Soon, with Your Help...

THE NEW ZOO

The Campaign to Make

Roger Williams Park Zoo

Exceptionally Great (Again).

A $35 million invitation to make something happen. Make your donor the real hero of the story. Shift the burden for achieving success to their shoulders, as here: "Coming Soon, with Your Help" thanks a lot." The donors are firmly consigned to the sidelines, cheering the team on.

Donors are the foundation on which programs and missions stand. They are investors hoping to change and improve the world through their gifts. They are not merely an inconvenient source of cash.

The donor-*centric* way of addressing supporters puts the donor first and foremost: "With your help, all these amazing things happened. And without your help, they won't." Here, the donors are the most important players on the field. They deserve to be on the field, key players on your team. Let's face it: without charitable investment, many organizations would shrink or sink.

27

The Cherry on Top

Being straightforward is one approach; kind of uninteresting, though.

I like to add surprises for the reader. It's a habit I picked up from two of my backgrounds: advertising and magazine journalism.

From advertising, to paraphrase the pioneering great, David Ogilvy: *You will never bore anyone into buying your cause.*

As for magazine journalism, it's all about entertaining readers while you inform them. In that order: entertainment first, *then* information. Otherwise, people stop reading. It doesn't take all that much, either, to be entertaining to readers: the occasional action verb, an overturned expectation or two, a few details that paint a vivid mental picture, or a splash of dialogue.

Jerry Panas says, "Our job [as case writers] is to add the salt. The taste." I call it putting a cherry on top.

A few examples of the cherry on top:

• The case for the French-American School of Rhode Island, meant for local, mostly monolingual, parents, has bilingual headlines inside, with the French prominent and the English translation in parentheses beneath.

• Most photos chosen for Roger Williams Park Zoo make eye

L'éducation bilingue est-elle vraiment 'le placement idéal'? Nombreux sont ceux qui le pensent. Cependant les frais de scolarité seuls ne suffi sent pas à couvrir tous les besoins de l'école.

Notre avenir dépend de votre générosité.

Is dual-language really "the best education money can buy?" Many think so. But tuition alone won't buy everything this school needs. Our future depends on your generosity.

What are the "cherries on top"? They're the entertainment values in your case. A school intrigues using bilingual headlines in mostly monolingual America....

Unforgettable Africa: Never Closer

And...in our New Zoo:

An elephant nursery

A larger "great outdoors" elephant yard

New feeding and viewing stations

A new elephant bathing pool

And...an elephant "spa"

The Campaign to Make Roger Williams Park Zoo Exceptionally Great (Again).

...and a zoo renovation emphasizes its new, more intimate exhibits with this rarely seen close up of an elephant's eye. School photos by Ron Cowie, www.rwcowie.com.

contact with the reader. But that's not all: elephants, the reader discovers, have six-inch long eyelashes!

The cover of the Us Helping Us case poses a stark, serious question over the head shots of two very attractive young adults: *What do you imagine is the number one killer here in D.C. of men and women like these? Guess again!*

The case for Colgate's endowed chairs campaign has a silhouetted photo of a unique chair tucked without comment into a corner of each spread. The weird chairs make the droll, visual point that the people occupying endowed chairs are one-of-a-kind scholars.

The case for the Tucson Symphony proclaims the counter-intuitive in a bold headline: *Strangely enough, developing a structural deficit is actually a good thing, in the world of top professional orchestras.* Turning lemons into lemonade is always an entertaining feat.

28

The Call to Action

At some point, you have to come right out and ask for the gift. That's your call to action. Do not leave "the ask" either unsaid or too elusive.

In a donor-centric world, all the credit for achieving – not just the cash goal but the essential, vital, urgent mission of the campaign – goes exclusively to the people who say yes.

For the prospect, therefore, the ask can be the most emotionally satisfying part of the case. With the ask, after all, the prospect steps into the picture and becomes the hero of the story (assuming she responds affirmatively to your case). A full-bodied ask – one that sets a dramatic stage onto which the prospect can step and be transformed – feels extra good, unlike anything else.

The ask in a case doesn't have to be long, either. "Be brief, be brilliant, be gone" is sage advice for any presentation.

Jerry Weissman mentions an especially graceful way to make an ask in his remarkable book, *Presenting to Win: The Art of Telling Your Story*. He describes how, at the very end of a company's presentation to stock investors, the speaker said:

XYZ Corporation is positioned to grow as a company. We invite you to join us in that growth.

Each year, The Bridge has to raise nearly half a million dollars in charitable gifts to continue mending lives.

And then there's our seedling endowment.

WHY WE NEED YOUR HELP NOW

The Bridge is nearly half a million dollars short.

Every year.

And that's not a deficit. That's the piece of our budget we have to raise annually from our cherished individual supporters, corporate sponsors, and charitable funders.

From you, in other words.

What kind of impact does your money buy?

Last year we served about 10,000 kids and parents, from West Hartford and other area towns. In just 12 months, thousands of school kids in West Hartford alone attended at least one Bridge-run anti-drug, youth development, adventure-aided learning, anger management, leadership, summer recreation, teen center, counseling, or shelter program.

Thousands of school kids.

Plus all those desperate, troubled families who get the help they need to hope again ... thanks to you and other supporters of The Bridge and its mission.

YOU'LL BE GLAD TO HEAR WE'RE GROWING

The Bridge recently increased our staff by 50 percent. Why?

Because our programs for children and families work, so towns want us to do more with their ever-changing problems. And we are. We've added specialists like a child and adolescent psychiatrist. We've opened three more shelters for girls and one for boys.

We're growing by leaps and bounds, to keep up with the complex and stressful world where we live and raise our kids.

Founded in 1969, The Bridge is here to stay. While we are a charity, we've sustained ourselves through four decades by being well-managed and professional. Be assured: your gift to The Bridge is a great investment in your community.

WE'LL ALSO HAVE A ROSY FUTURE, WITH YOUR HELP

There are many ways you can support the mission of The Bridge. You could, for instance, support our future.

Allow us to introduce our new endowment fund.

It's a permanent endowment, which means we never spend the principal, only a portion of the annual income – the rest gets plowed back into growth.

Let's face it. We're in the "troubled family, troubled youth" business.

While we'd love to see all the problems mended and gone, that's just not true to life. The Bridge will always be needed.

The Hartford Foundation for Public Giving, one of the country's oldest, largest, and most successful community foundations – and a long-time supporter of The Bridge – manages our new permanent endowment.

Please consider giving now to the endowment – or adding a gift in your will. Donors who make a planned gift to support our future will be permanently recognized as members of our new Planned Giving Society, *Builders for the Future*.

Be The Bridge. Support The Bridge. Give a much-needed helping hand to your community's children and families.

In this case for support, the funding requirement becomes an annual challenge. As government puts fewer and fewer dollars into community social service, it can become the donors' responsibility (and pleasure) to pick up the torch. The majority of donors see social service charities as the only "real" charities, recent research revealed

---

WASHINGTON, D.C.—EPICENTER OF THE U.S. HIV/AIDS EPIDEMIC WHERE AT THE CURRENT MOMENT...

- The rate of HIV infection, the precursor to AIDS, is higher here than in any other major metropolitan area in the U.S. (three times higher than in San Francisco).

- AIDS has become the leading cause of death among BLACK MEN AGES 35–44 and among BLACK WOMEN AGES 25–44, regardless of sexual preference.

- The rate of new AIDS cases is the highest of any major U.S. city.

- 33% of those who are HIV infected don't realize they have the disease.

- 80% of those living with AIDS are black.

- The incidence of AIDS per capita is the highest in America.

Do you find these facts disturbing? Good. They are. Are you searching for a way to reduce HIV infection here in D.C.? Even better.

Time to write a check!

Angry enough after reading these horrifying facts? "Time to write a check!" the case for an upgraded HIV clinic strongly suggests.

Perfect. Here's how I used the same formulation for a school, over the signature of the board chair:

XYZ School offers a very attractive opportunity to change the future of childhood education in Boston. I invite you to join us.

Then there's this approach, which links the donor's participation directly to a major achievement. The following statement is the lead-in for a national campaign (confidentiality requires me to conceal the client's name):

The [organization's name] and the end of global warming.
Give us your help and seven years.

Making the ask, i.e., calling for action, at the end of your case provides the reader with two things she will need: (1) clear direction

131

THE CAMPAIGN FOR PERMANENT ENDOWMENT: CODA

Dear lover of live classical music...

A few closing words from Marie Langlois about the urgent need for endowment:

"THE PHILHARMONIC TOOK THE RISK OF INVESTING OVER THE LAST DECADE so that Rhode Islanders could experience great symphonic sound, the best regional orchestra in America.

"We took the risk of merging with the Music School, because we saw that music education was being dropped in many schools. We didn't want that to disappear.

"We took these risks because we thought people would respond. And they did!

"But there is still one missing piece in our financial plan: a strong, permanent endowment.

"We need that to guarantee our long-term financial viability. We cannot make the numbers work without an endowment. If we don't establish one now, we risk wasting the investment everyone has made in this Philharmonic over the past 50 years.

"Thank you for believing with me in the future of symphonic music in Rhode Island."

Marie Langlois, Board member and past president of the Rhode Island Philharmonic

And while we have your ear, we'd like to play for you a variation on an old Cole Porter tune ...

Begin the Bequest

NEXT TIME YOU'RE THINKING ABOUT YOUR LEGACY — about the things you think matter in life — remember all those times when live music swept you away ... and changed your world. And give that gift to the next generation of music lovers, and the one after that, in perpetuity, by including a bequest to the Rhode Island Philharmonic's Permanent Endowment in your estate.

What a way to be remembered: You kept the music alive.

LARRY RACHLEFF PHOTOGRAPH BY JIM EGAN
ORCHESTRA, CARNEGIE HALL AND ALL MUSIC SCHOOL STUDENT PHOTOGRAPHS BY WENDY R. LITKE

A past president, well known in the community for her success as an investment advisor, sanctions the campaign.

(as in, "What exactly do you want me to do?"; and (2) emotional satisfaction (as in, "My choice to become a donor is a real opportunity to change the world.").

29

The Role of Visuals

The purpose of photos and other visuals is to:

1) Grab attention ruthlessly. We know from Siegfried Vögele's research that the human eye can't resist looking at pictures.

2) Melt the heart instantly, no words needed.

Consider the cover for the French-American School of Rhode Island case. The designer presented the school with a half dozen ideas. The example shown on the left was one of the rejects. Why was the example on the right given the go-ahead? For several reasons, all of them having to do with the murky workings of psychology:

1) There's the "cuteness factor." In biology, cuteness has a function: it's how adults of a species recognize that their offspring still need care. We all respond to cute: it's hardwired into the human brain. Kids (puppies and kittens, too) raise a ton of money. This cover had the cuteness factor; the others didn't.

2) There's the angle of the photo, looking down at the adorable child, putting the viewer in a position of dominance. This is a good thing, this position of dominance. It reminds us subliminally that we're the ones who have to help this child.

3) There's Dr. Siegfried Vogele's influence, once again. Among

Shown above, one of several also-ran designs for a case cover.

Shown here, the winning cover, with its psychological depths. Winning cover photo by Ron Cowie, www.rwcowie.com.

other significant findings, his eye motion studies discovered that photos of eyes attract our eyes, involuntarily. We can't not look. The girl's big eyes are a winner.

All the other covers were pretty enough. But none of them was *psychologically* persuasive.

Of course, there is one other thing visuals can do for your case, if you are publishing a nicely designed, photographically rich brochure. Professional-grade visuals grant you "the front-end spit and polish that a successful brand requires," as *The Economist* magazine once put it.

30

"I'll Know a Great Case When I See It"

A while back the phone rang. The head of publications at a distinguished urban university was on the line. She had a problem she hoped I could fix.

For a solid year, a capital campaign case had circulated inside her school without gaining final approval. Many well-groomed hands – the president, deans, faculty members – had touched it with red pen and comment. The case was now on version #6 and had stretched to 33 single-spaced pages. And it still wasn't right. Could I give it a look and maybe salvage it?

The answer was yes and no.

Yes, I gave it a look. Yes, I made sense of the project, inserting a decent rationale and ladling in sufficient emotional hooks. Yes, I wrote some framing language that made it easier to navigate this vast document. Yes, I trimmed out the repetitious verbiage. Yes, I answered the prospect's three big questions.

I boast high standards. And by those standards, this case, when I finished with it, was ready to go out into the world and help the university raise money.

But could I *salvage* it? No.

Because the powers that be didn't approve my version either. Every case writer has a sad story like this. The approval process for cases is often built for failure, not success.

■ Looking through the right set of eyes

In an ideal world, the fundraising chief *alone* approves the final language of the case, once all the various stakeholders' opinions have been gathered and weighed. In an ideal world, that well-trained fundraising chief controls all the levers relevant to achieving success in her job.

That's the ideal. It's not a high ideal, either; merely a reasonable one.

And then there's the world we live in, where reason often takes a frustrated back seat to untutored opinion, forceful egos, caprice, and office politics. Case statements can be especially tough to write at universities, where a culture of consensus asks, honors, and accommodates every opinion.

There is among non-professionals the expectation that "I'll know a good case when I read it."

Maybe. But don't count on it.

Without training in the fine arts of persuasion and donor communications, insiders (volunteers as well as staff) tend to view a case through the wrong set of eyes. Insider eyes are not outsider eyes.

Most prospects won't see your project the way you see it.

You will have your well-framed and perfectly logical reasons for wanting to do what you want to do. All you're missing is philanthropic support. Your inclination will be to write about what you know best: the details of your project. You will seek "to educate the donor."

Across the desk is the prospect. The person might be a bit of an insider: a former board member, an alum, an art lover, a grateful patient perhaps. Or maybe not. What you consider most important, the reasons behind the project and its details, may be the least important aspects of the case for the donor. Sure, your project has to make sense; inane projects don't attract support. But *your* reasons for seeking support are not necessarily *their* reasons for giving support.

Their reasons are emotional. Psychological. And cases often ignore or skimp on those reasons.

Insiders want to talk about plans. Nuts and bolts. Details.

But people don't give to your nuts and bolts. They give to your promise. Your mission. Your vision. The thing you're trying to bring into the world.

Outsiders want to feel their best heart beating. They want to feel how good they are, how special they are, what a difference they're making to the world – through giving to your campaign.

Since they're writing the checks, ask yourself, whose reasons matter more: yours or theirs?

31

Reality Check

*A less-than-great case
won't kill your capital campaign*

This book is *not* just for organizations engaging in capital campaigns. All organizations that depend on philanthropy need a case for support under the hood.

But for a moment I'd like to speak directly to those who *are* attempting a run at a big-bucks goal.

Relax.

A case statement that does not tell its story thrillingly well will *not* kill a capital campaign; assuming your solicitors have true passion for the project, and you've chosen your prospects well.

I know a university that raised a third of its $300 million goal with no case at all on paper. The school had something far more effective: a visionary, articulate president speaking about giving opportunities to a handful of well-qualified people.

And a handful it will be, for most of the money. Guy Mallabone, vice president of external relations at SAIT Polytechnic in Calgary, in 2008 estimated that 97 percent of his goal derived from just 3 percent of his donors.

The case by itself does not make the sale. In a capital campaign, there are other, far more important factors involved: the personal interests and priorities of your prospects, their respect for the individuals who solicit them, the philanthropic opportunity your project represents, and such.

Compton International, counsel for more than 1,000 capital campaigns worldwide, drew up a list of 20 reasons why major donors give. Chief among the motivations: "Because someone they know and respect asks them to give."

Was there a case statement involved? Certainly, if the campaign was professionally managed. But did the case statement get the gift? No. The peer-to-peer approach got the gift. The case played no more than a supporting role, there to provide details and background.

So take a breath. Don't let the writing of a case intimidate you. A below-average case in the hands of an above-average peer-to-peer solicitor will still bring in cash.

Afterword

With the process I teach in this book, you can write an urgent, compelling case for pretty much any organization.

I wasn't born knowing this process. Parts of it I learned from other case writers, eminent ones like Jerry Panas, Ron Arena, and Brigitte Mertling. Some I learned from a ten-year stretch writing freelance magazine articles.

A good case and a good magazine piece share key similarities. Both kinds of writing try to anticipate the audience's questions and answer them convincingly. Both use information, surprise and entertainment to persuade.

The process taught in this book has an ulterior motive: it forces you to see your organization, its mission and projects, through an outsider's – rather than insider's – eyes. You need that perspective. Staff and board are hobbled by what Chip and Dan Heath, authors of *Made To Stick*, call "the curse of knowledge." You know too much for your own good.

During the year or so while I wrote this book, I worked on nine cases. Their campaign goals totaled nearly $400 million. The clients ranged in size from a major research university to a city symphony to a local child service agency. I used the same process for each of them. Thanks to the process, I always uncovered a powerful story packed with appeal for prospective donors.

It's not the fastest process in the world; you'll devote a week or more to the research and writing, all told. But it is a simple process anyone, including those who are not professional writers, can follow successfully.

There's a great case waiting to be written.

And you're going to be the writer.

Acknowledgements

Many organizations and experts appear in this book, teaching by their examples and experience. Some know me. Some have no idea I exist or how much I respect them. All have my unbounded thanks. They are the miracle fibers that give the book its validity. They include:

The Antiquarian and Landmarks Society; Ron Arena, Marts & Lundy; the Audubon Society of Rhode Island; The Bridge; Jeff Brooks, Merkle/Domain; Capital Quest; Robert Cialdini; Colgate University; Compton International; Community Foundation for Southeast Michigan; Connecticut Community for Addiction Recovery; French-American School of Rhode Island; Kay Sprinkel Grace; Greenpoint Graphics; Jeff Hall; Kris Hermanns; Hospice of the Chesapeake; Housatonic Youth Service Bureau; Dianna Huff; Johnson, Grossnickle and Associates; Simone Joyaux; George Lakoff; League of Women Voters; Manchester Area Conference of Churches; Brigitte C. Mertling; Kristine Merz; My Sister's Place; National Center for Lesbian Rights; Northeast Design; David Ogilvy; Orange Square; Jerry Panas; Poynter Institute; Paul Pribbenow; Jim Rattray; Rhode Island Philharmonic; Rick Schwartz; Several Sources Foundation; Shasta Community Health Center; George Smith; Southcoast Health System; Tucson Symphony; Us Helping Us; Siegfried Vögele; Volunteers in Providence Schools; Mal Warwick; The Wheeler School; Stanley Weinstein; Jerry Weissman; Maureen Welch; Jeremy Wells; the Women's Fund of Rhode Island.

Appendix

The Five Dirty Secrets
of Capital Campaigns

*Steve Manzi, a senior executive at Changing Our World, Inc., a major
fundraising consultancy based in New York City, penned the following
good advice a few years back. It puts capital campaign case statements
in perspective.*

*You might well wonder, given Steve Manzi's dismissive Secret No. 2,
why a case statement is worth the trouble at all. Don't be fooled. Going
through the process of creating a case – forcing yourself to see your mission
or campaign through an outsider's eyes – is essential. A case is how you
and your solicitors discover why you're really raising money.*

Been holding them in for years. Can't refrain any longer. Must
disclose the truths that are burning inside. Never before spoken out
loud, they are..."The Five Dirty Secrets of Capital Campaigns." Read
them once; commit them to memory; and then destroy this before
anyone else sees it.

1) Campaigns Are Won or Lost Before They Start

The Campaign Planning Phase - which should begin well in
advance of any potential campaign - is the essential building block
upon which successful campaigns are built. This phase includes a
number of components, including the establishment of institutional
priorities, financial planning, internal consensus building, initial case
development, lead prospect identification, and a campaign feasibility
study.

While each of these activities involves tremendous work, and a
lot of discussions, the most important element during each step is
listening. Is there agreement on and, more importantly, enthusiasm
for the case? Is the financial goal based on what you're hearing through
the feasibility study, or is it based on what the institution wants or
needs? In essence, the chief objective of the planning stage is to

develop credible plans and credible responses to any issues major gift prospects may throw your way when you finally get out there and ask.

2) The Myth of the Campaign Case Statement Publication

We agonize over the wording. We go head-to-head with the designers. We spend sleepless nights fretting over the printer. We live in secret shame, hoping that no one else will notice the typo in paragraph two on page seven.

But you know what? Almost nobody really reads the Case Statement.

Just to be clear, I'm not suggesting that we don't need them, or that we shouldn't spend time making sure they read well and look good. What I am suggesting, though, is that they be viewed as what they are: a useful campaign tool. The most superb Case Statement in the world, no matter how impressive, can't raise money by itself.

Here's a suggestion: reduce your time spent worrying about the Case by 10%, and devote that time to accelerating a leadership gift ask. An early "top of the gift table" close will ultimately have a bigger impact on the Campaign than even a top-notch Case Statement booklet.

3) Charismatic Leaders Trump Strong Cases

Strong cases presented by weak executives or volunteer leaders face an uphill battle. Regrettably, the converse is true as well: you can raise a lot of money for a mediocre case if the leaders are passionate. The bottom line is that people are ultimately more important than the case: donors are considerably more likely to invest their charitable dollars when they believe in and are inspired by an institution's leadership.

How can you best motivate campaign leadership to do the things they may least be inclined to do? Read on.

4) The Single Major Factor Behind Most Successful Campaigns is...

... a pervasive sense of optimism.

Yes. I am channeling the spirits of Norman Vincent Peale and Dale Carnegie (they're also giving me tips on next week's MegaLotto numbers, but I'll deal with that another time).

Campaigns succeed when people believe they will succeed. You already know that to be true, by virtue of the way campaigns are designed: you don't take them public until you have raised sufficient funds in the private phase, and you have clearly mapped out where the rest of the money is coming from. Prospective donors need to believe that they are contributing to a winning enterprise.

As the fundraising professional involved with the campaign, the optimism has to originate with you: you're the one who has to initially impart the sense of inevitable success to the organizational and campaign leadership. If you do, you'll find that your campaign leaders will be more likely to make the calls, to set up the campaign visits, and to reflect that optimism when making the ask.

5) The Single Major Factor Behind Most Failed Campaigns is...

... the leaders were afraid to ask. They procrastinate in making calls and in setting appointments, and when they finally get to the solicitation, they don't put a specific gift amount on the table.

Compare this with the single most successful capital campaign I ever directed. Throughout the campaign, I met weekly with the institution's president to review priority prospects and requests under consideration; after going through the list, she would immediately - in front of me - pick up the phone and call each of them to set-up or follow up on a visit. In fact, she knew that she would be spending her summer holiday in the same seaside community as a somewhat elusive major prospect, so she made a particular point of driving each day past his vacation home until she spied him in the yard, and was able to stop and speak to him.

Even I was a little apprehensive about this guerilla approach, but the president was a nun and figured that no jury would ever convict her of stalking. Besides which, it worked: we got the gift. So the secrets are out - and I might as well come clean with my true feelings about Capital Campaigns.

Yes, they're a lot of hard work, they require intricate planning, and no matter what I say, you – and I – are still going to worry about them day and night from the launch all the way up until the final pledge payment is received. But they'll also give you an incredible kick when you land the initial leadership gifts, when you surpass your interim goals, and when the venerable fundraising thermometer reaches the boiling point.

Savor those moments - you and your team have earned them!

Read These Two Books, Too

The experts who, I believe, know the most about presenting your case do not write for a nonprofit audience. They write for business. The two best books on cases that I've read are both business books, and both bestsellers: *Made to Stick*, by the Bros. Heath; and *Presenting to Win*, by Jerry Weissman.

• *Made to Stick*

Made to Stick, written by a Stanford business professor and a former Harvard Business School researcher, argues that lasting, persuasive messages share six qualities. Each quality is individually penetrating; in combination, they are wickedly, almost irresistibly, powerful.

The qualities are: simplicity, unexpectedness, concreteness, credibility, having emotional content, and speaking in stories. I picked up *Made to Stick* (published 2007) to relax, just as I was finishing the book you're reading. One chapter in, I was openly cheering.

Chip and Dan Heath have written the book all professional communicators (and that bunch includes *all* fundraisers, executive directors, and board chairs) MUST!!! read. I can promise you, I'll be using *Made to Stick* principles for the rest of my career to help my case clients attract millions in gifts from delighted donors. How about you?

• *Presenting to Win*

The other book, *Presenting to Win*, was one of those how-to books that sounds like it's about something small (PowerPoint presentations would be one wrong guess); when in fact it's about something huge: persuading a skeptical, analytical audience (in this case, venture capitalists and stock market analysts) that your idea is wonderful and deserves millions of dollars in support.

The author's back story is revealing. Jerry Weissman had been a television producer for CBS and a screenwriter. Then an old college buddy who'd become a top venture capitalist called, asking for help. He wanted Weissman to improve a road show for an initial public offering (IPO) of stock.

It wouldn't be easy. And the pressure was crushing. "Succeeding in an IPO road show is the ultimate example of winning over the toughest crowd. The investors are both demanding and knowledgeable, the stakes are high, and a swing of one dollar in the share price of the offering translates into millions."

As a dismayed Weissman discovered while watching others present their typical IPO road shows, "The problem is that nobody knows how to tell a story. And what's worse, nobody *knows* that they don't know how to tell a story!"

Learn to tell your story perfectly. Read his book, *Presenting to Win*.

The Case for
Alzheimer's Disease International

Vision for Development

The following example, presented in full in the next 10 pages, is case writing at a high level.

It is clear and easy to follow. It is comprehensive without excess. It uses photography brilliantly (notice the cover, where the faded snapshot comes back into focus). It is about giving hope a fighting chance against a disease that will wreck millions of families a year around the world, if left unchecked.

Note: This is a vision statement, as the title declares. A campaign case is usually a vision statement. Often, a case for annual support is more about mission than vision. Mistake? A bit. Don't overlook the power of vision to move your annual supporters, too.

Growth should be part of your everlasting plan. Donors find it rewarding emotionally to invest in growth. Investing is your agency's mere subsistence is emotionally null.

Reprinted by permission, courtesy of Jon Duschinsky, director, Bethechange Consulting. Design by Bastien Larriaga, copy and concept by Jon Duschinsky. Client: Alzheimer's Disease International - Director Marc Wortmann.

Vision for **development**

Fighting for a better quality of life
for people around the world

Alzheimer's Disease International

A "Vision For Development"

The Programmes

ADI's programmes are the result of **23 years' of experience** in helping drive forward the fight against Alzheimer's around the world. They have proven their effectiveness, and their impact is an incredible positive multiplier for national associations, people with dementia and carers around the world.

The need for these programmes and services is greatest in countries that have the smallest financial capacity. That is why ADI is launching "**VISION FOR DEVELOPMENT**", a new fundraising campaign designed to increase the impact of ADI's programmes around the world. The campaign will have three objectives:

- **Develop research programmes** to understand the prevalence and impact of Alzheimer's in low and middle income countries (where two-thirds of people with dementia live) through the "10/66 Research Programme"

- **Provide systematic opportunities for learning** and support of implementation to organisations, especially in developing countries, through 'Alzheimer University' and the unique 'Twinning programme'

- **Increase awareness of the impact of dementia** by reinforcing the reach of 'World Alzheimer's Day' and the impact of the annual ADI Conference

Alzheimer University

This is a series of **practical workshops** aimed at helping staff and volunteers of Alzheimer associations build and strengthen capacity and develop their organisations. The promise is that after a week at Alzheimer University, **each participant will go home with the knowledge of how to develop Alzheimer support groups**, organise governance, run best practice programmes and increase the impact of the fight against the disease. ADI has already run ten successful Alzheimer University training programmes that have been attended by 68 countries.

Twinning

Twinning is a formal, two-way partnership between two Alzheimer associations. It is an opportunity for capacity building within two associations, giving them the chance to work together to resolve organisational issues. The established national Alzheimer association has knowledge, experience and resources which can be shared with the developing association to enable it to reach a level of provision and performance that directly benefits people with dementia. **The programme has so far involved 12 countries** that have sought mutual benefit from the establishment of a formal alliance through which best practice can be shared. ADI financially supports site visits between the two associations and provides materials, guidance and a clear set of goals with which to measure progress.

Annual international conference

ADI holds the longest running annual international conference on dementia. **The conference is unique in that it brings together everyone with an interest in dementia** – people with dementia, families, health and care professionals, researchers and staff and volunteers of Alzheimer associations from around the world. In the last few years, conferences have been held in Germany, Turkey and Japan. The 2007 Conference is to be held in Caracas, Venezuela.

World Alzheimer's Day

World Alzheimer's Day, **celebrated on September 21 each year**, was launched in 1994 with support from the World Health Organization to mark ADI's tenth anniversary. It is an opportunity to raise global awareness about dementia and its impact on families and the important work of our members throughout the world. ADI coordinates World Alzheimer's Day and **provides members with a free tool kit and campaign materials** to help them organise their own events.

![Alzheimer's Disease International logo]

Alzheimer's Disease International

The **Programmes** /
How you can **help**

The 10/66 Dementia Research Group

ADI's 10/66 Dementia Research Group gets its name from the fact that 66% of people with dementia live in developing countries, but less than 10% of all research is directed towards them. Over one hundred researchers from 32 developing countries have contributed to the work of this unique network over the last eight years. Prevalence and incidence studies, and randomised controlled trials are now underway in 10 countries in Latin America, Africa, South and South East Asia. The group has had its work published in leading journals including The Lancet and presents its research findings at major international conferences. However, more and better services for people with dementia can only be secured through raising public awareness and influencing policy. The new evidence on the growing numbers of people with dementia, the impact on families and on society, the limited access to health and social care, and the potential benefits of interventions is a powerful tool for advocacy. Our motto is 'putting research to work'. ADI is working closely with the 10/66 investigators to prepare media information packs, press releases and policy briefings based on key research findings. 10/66 data will in future be incorporated into an authoritative ADI-sponsored World Dementia Report.

The World's Alzheimer Resource

ADI produces a range of publications – a website, newsletter, fact sheets, booklets and a video for primary care doctors about dementia – for members and for the general public. Most of the materials are available in Spanish and English and are usually free of charge. ADI also has an intranet site for members.

HOW YOU CAN HELP

ADI is seeking funding from organisations and individuals who understand the importance of the issues surrounding ageing, and who share its vision of a world without dementia.

Through its unique membership structure, ADI is in the position to bring great value, knowledge and shared experience to its supporters as well as its beneficiaries.

All supporters of the "VISION FOR DEVELOPMENT" campaign will of course receive full and regular impact reports on all programmes, showing the tangible results of work being carried out around the world on the lives of those who need it most.

In addition, ADI is very pleased to be able to offer its supporters recognition opportunities that will include:

Widespread brand recognition for supporters on the Campaign communication profile (online and offline) that will be distributed internationally

Unrivalled visibility at the annual ADI conference, as well as presence at high-profile gala events

A rare opportunity to gain regular access to national Alzheimer associations from around the world at ADI's Alzheimer University courses

A seat on the prestigious ADI "Vision for Development" Campaign Committee

Vision for development

Through its programmes, ADI has created a global movement of scientists, people with dementia, carers and leaders who are moving forward together and tackling the diseases caused by ageing on every level. The movement strengthens both people and organisations by helping to show that there are real solutions to their problems. It provides support and advice and shows that no one is alone with dementia.

Alzheimer's Disease International

Alzheimer's Disease International
64 Great Suffolk Street
London
SE1 0BL
UK

Tel: +44 20 79810880
Fax: +44 20 79282357
Email: info@alz.co.uk

Website: www.alz.co.uk/

Alzheimer University

THE OBJECTIVES OF THE "VISION FOR DEVELOPMENT" CAMPAIGN

To meet the huge demand for knowledge and support from the growing network of Alzheimer associations around the world, ADI will increase the number of Universities from 2 to 4 annually. These two additional learning events will respectively focus on raising funds for Alzheimer associations, and raising awareness of the disease.

To achieve this, ADI will raise
$1.25 million
over 5 years

Outline

The Alzheimer University is a **training programme** that ADI offers to Alzheimer associations to increase participants' awareness and skills of how to set up and run an association. It is also a unique opportunity for more established associations to review and consolidate their aims and expertise, to identify and fill gaps in their skills and knowledge and to become more effective in mission delivery.

Aims

The immediate aims of the Alzheimer University workshops are to:
- Give participants **information and guidance** in the proven skills of establishing and running an Alzheimer organisation
- Enable participants to **share** past and present **experiences** of developing and running their association
- **Increase** the organisational competence and **professionalism** of participants' associations
- Equip participants with skills and **knowledge to formulate a strategy** to further develop their association and ensure wider reach and impact

Methods

Alzheimer University courses run over 2-3 days and contain both **presentations** and **group activities** to ensure dynamic and maximum learning. Speakers are invited from a range of developed organisations, other Alzheimer associations, professional bodies and international charities to share their experience and expertise.

Impact

Since the first Alzheimer University in 1998, ADI has organised ten of these highly successful programmes, bringing tangible and effective benefit to Alzheimer associations around the world and **advancing the international dementia movement.**

Two programmes are held annually - one on advocacy and policy and another for emerging associations. Seven developing countries attended the University in April 2007 and over 20 countries attended the University in Milwaukee in July 2007 on public policy and advocacy. ADI has even developed a Spanish language course for its Latin American members

Twinning

Alzheimer's Disease International

THE OBJECTIVES OF THE "VISION FOR DEVELOPMENT" CAMPAIGN

ADI will increase the number of twins to 10 by the end of 2008 and will support them until 2012. Support will be provided including:

- Advice on funding applications and guidelines
- Information on action planning and evaluation forms
- Guidance and evaluation
- Financial support for the visits and exchange systems

To achieve this, ADI will raise **$500k** over 5 years

Outline

Together, ADI's members have much expertise about caring for and supporting people with dementia and their carers. The ADI Twinning Programme aims to **harness this knowledge** and disseminate it throughout the world through an innovative two-way relationship between Alzheimer organisations in developing and developed countries.

Aims

The ultimate aim is to ensure that people with dementia and their carers receive the best **quality care and support**, regardless of where they live. It is an opportunity for collaboration between Alzheimer associations, giving them the chance to work together to resolve organisational issues and increase the mission delivery and impact of their organisations.

The benefits of twinning include capacity building, information sharing, building relationships and promoting global solidarity.

Twinning is not one association giving to another in need; both associations gain from the relationship, work together, share information and gain insight and operational capacity as a result.

Methods

Following an application process, associations are paired to ensure resources are used effectively and to enhance cultural sensitivity, knowledge and communication. The twinned associations then organise regular visits and exchanges to collect information and implement an action plan of realistic and specific objectives to be achieved during the twinning period.

Impact

The ADI Twinning Programme is currently supporting 6 twins (12 Alzheimer associations) for a three-year period. **Successes so far**:

- **A demonstration Day Care Centre** has been established in Lahore, Pakistan. It was planned with assistance from a visiting staff member from Alzheimer's Australia Western Australia who also educated the association staff.
- The Alzheimer Society of Canada have set up a successful and cost effective way of shipping resources to the Alzheimer's Society of Trinidad and Tobago. This means that Trinidad and Tobago has accurate and up to date information, which is driving its efficiency and impact locally.

Alzheimer's Disease International

Annual international conference

THE OBJECTIVES OF THE "VISION FOR DEVELOPMENT" CAMPAIGN

In order to meet the need for information transfer and best practice in all elements of the fight against Alzheimer's, ADI will run annual conferences with 2 000 delegates and increase accessibility for organisations from developing countries.

*ADI will achieve these objectives by making the Conference **self-funding** by 2009*

Outline

ADI's conference is unique in the international dementia conference field. Recognised for its depth of content and education, the event provides an interdisciplinary programme for professionals in dementia care, people with dementia, family carers, medical professionals and researchers, in addition to attracting Alzheimer associations and people interested in setting up Alzheimer associations.

Aims

The strategic aims of the conference are:

- To **promote** ADI's key messages and campaigns
- To **build** the event into the recognised international platform for networking and exchange of best practice in dementia care
- To **support members** and potential members in the region where the conference takes place.

Impact

Close to 7 000 participants from around the world have participated in the ADI Annual Conference since 2004. **The nomadic nature of the event** ensures that best practice shared during the conference is effectively disseminated to improve the quality of life for people with dementia and their carers globally.

World Alzheimer's Day™ and Campaigning

THE OBJECTIVES OF THE "VISION FOR DEVELOPMENT" CAMPAIGN

Awareness is one of the major issues limiting the fight against Alzheimer's worldwide. Therefore, ADI will start a global awareness campaign using the vehicle of World Alzheimer's Day as a key focal point. Through media and lobbying, both internationally and nationally (by the ADI membership), the campaign will target the general public as well as general practitioners in order to increase diagnosis of the disease and put more people with dementia on the road to treatment.

To achieve this, ADI will raise **$1 million** over 5 years

Outline

ADI organises World Alzheimer's Day on 21st September. Each year this international collective campaign provides **ADI members around the world** a platform to organise media events and lobbying activities to bring dementia to the attention of governments, opinion leaders, medical professionals and the general public.

Method

ADI produces a toolkit and campaign materials to help members make the most of the day. The toolkit suggests ideas for events, gives practical advice on how to organise activities and how to secure media attention. Publicity materials including posters, stickers, balloons and postcards are produced in both English and Spanish. They can also be translated and used in other languages. Printed materials including background on the disease and media information kits are also provided as well as electronic versions of the materials, which are made available to adapt and download from the ADI intranet site.

Impact

World Alzheimer's Day campaigns have resulted in real tangible benefits for people with dementia and their families. In 2006, more than 60 countries participated by holding media campaigns, Memory Walks and mass memory testing. Some of the successes of World Alzheimer's Day:

- **Mexico** - Collaboration with the Secretary of Health to develop 160 training courses for doctors in the country's main cities
- **Malta** - Memory Walk in Malta on World Alzheimer's Day
- **India** - Charter of rights for people with dementia and their carers released by The Minister for Social Justice and Empowerment
- **Turkey** - The opening of Turkey's first nursing home for people with dementia prompted a Mayor from a nearby city to build a nursing home in his own city.

Method

The 10/66 population-based surveys involve **large scale epidemiological studies** of all residents aged 65 years and over in defined urban and rural districts. All older participants are screened for the presence of cognitive impairment, dementia, stroke, diabetes, hypertension, depression and other major disabling health conditions. A blood sample is collected, and a relative interviewed about care arrangements. All participants from the baseline survey are then followed up three years later, in an incidence phase. The baseline survey data is being used to measure prevalence (and numbers), and the impact of dementia relative to other health conditions – on disability, needs for care, carer strain and economic cost. The follow-up study will identify risk factors for dementia (cardiovascular health, poor diet and genes), and to help us to understand the way that needs for support and care for people with dementia evolve over time. A carer intervention ('Helping Carers to Care') is being trialled in randomised controlled trials in seven centres – and has the potential to provide immediate and direct benefit.

Impact

The excellence of the 10/66 research programme has been validated through the award of major research grants from the Wellcome Trust, the US Alzheimer's Association, and the World Health Organization. Currently research is being undertaken in India, China, Cuba, Brazil, Dominican Republic, Peru, Mexico, Argentina, Venezuela and Nigeria. Over 19 000 individuals have participated so far. Key findings include

- The prevalence of dementia in low income countries seems to have been underestimated in previous studies
- Dementia has a much larger impact than other, physical, health conditions on needs for care, giving up work to care, and carer strain
- Few families seek help, and public and community health services are neither trained nor resourced to provide appropriate support them in the longer term
- Pensions are limited - people with dementia do not receive disability benefits, and carers do not receive financial compensation, although the costs of care are high
- More than half of all people with dementia in low-income countries live in three-generation households with one or more children under the age of 16.

The 10/66 programme has helped to develop local sustainable capacity for research, and to attract the brightest young graduates into academic and clinical careers that focus on older people's health. In every 10/66 centre there is now a core of young researchers, experienced in epidemiological research methods and in the clinical assessment of dementia and other mental disorders.

The World's Alzheimer's Resource

THE OBJECTIVES OF THE "VISION FOR DEVELOPMENT" CAMPAIGN

Centralising information and facilitating access to knowledge on dementia are essential to the fight against the disease, especially in developing countries. ADI is uniquely positioned to take on the challenge of building a global knowledge centre on dementia, one that is easily accessible and regularly updated.

To achieve this, ADI will raise **$500k**

Outline

ADI disseminates reliable and accurate information through its website and publications. ADI's information is a valuable resource for both the general public and Alzheimer associations.

Aims

ADI aims to produce publications, both online and offline, that help Alzheimer associations and other stakeholders in the field of dementia to keep abreast of the fight against the disease around the world. The ADI website offers readable information about Alzheimer's disease and dementia, including practical advice for carers and people with dementia.

Methods

Resources include a newsletter, fact sheets, booklets and a video for primary care doctors about dementia.

ADI's regular **newsletter,** Global Perspective, contains regular features including a carer's story, a research update and the 'living with dementia' section, aimed at people with dementia. The ADI **website** also features information about ADI and its activities, including past and future annual conferences and World Alzheimer's Day campaigns. The website has downloadable versions of ADI publications, contact details for Alzheimer associations around the world, and links to information about dementia in many languages other than English. The ADI intranet site has a range of documents and resources for member associations and others working with ADI.

ADI's most popular printed publication is the **Help for Caregivers booklet**, produced in collaboration with the World Health Organization. The booklet, aimed at family carers, contains information on dementia and provides practical tips on how to care for a person with dementia.

Impact

The resources, booklets and fact sheets produced by ADI constitute a primary information hub for people setting up and developing Alzheimer associations or working within the field around the world. Most ADI publications are available in English and Spanish, and some are available in additional languages. Wherever possible, ADI's printed booklets and fact sheets are provided free of charge.

ABOUT THE AUTHOR

Tom Ahern is the author of *How to Write Fundraising Materials that Raise More Money, Raising More Money with Newsletters than You Ever Thought Possible*, and *Keep Your Donors: The Guide to Better Communications & Stronger Relationships*.

He is in demand as a communications trainer, traveling internationally to present his workshops. He is an award-winning magazine journalist (which means he knows how to tell a story).

And he gets results. His work has won three prestigious Gold Quill awards, given annually to communications programs judged to be among the most effective in the world. He's written numerous cases for successful campaigns, totaling more than $1.5 billion (B as in Boy) in goals.

Other Books of Interest

How to Raise Planned Gifts by Mail, by Larry Stelter, 102 pp., $24.95.

While *executing* a planned gift can be complicated, that's irrelevant really. Attorneys, financial planners, and CPAs can and should handle the paperwork. Your job as staff is far simpler. Namely, *to instill interest* in making a planned gift. And Larry Stelter, who heads the largest planned giving marketing company in the U.S., shows you how to accomplish that *and* lay the groundwork for closing the gift.

Raising Thousands (if Not Tens of Thousands) of Dollars with Email, by Madeline Stanionis, 108 pp., $24.95.

After reading the title of this book, you're probably saying: "Sure, the American Red Cross can raise tons of money with email, but my agency isn't a brand name. You're telling me I can do the same!?" Well, no. But what Madeline Stanionis is saying is that you can raise a healthy amount if you use her proven approach to email fundraising.

Raising $1,000 Gifts by Mail, by Mal Warwick, 104 pp., $24.95.

Whoever heard of raising $1,000 gifts by mail? That's the realm of personal solicitation, right? Not exclusively, says Mal Warwick. He shows you - with carefully selected examples - how to succeed with high-dollar mail, walking you step by step through the process of identifying your prospects, crafting the right letter, the right brochure, the right response device, and the right envelope.

Emerson & Church, Publishers
www.emersonandchurch.com

The Gold Standard
In Books for Nonprofit Boards

Each can be read in an hour • Quantity discounts up to 50 percent

Fund Raising Realities Every Board Member Must Face
David Lansdowne, 112 pp., $24.95.

If every board member of every nonprofit organization in America read this book, it's no exaggeration to say that millions upon millions of additional dollars would be raised.

How could it be otherwise when, after spending just *one* hour with this gem, board members everywhere would understand virtually everything they need to know about raising major gifts. Not more, not less. Just exactly what they need to do to be successful.

In his book, *Fund Raising Realities Every Board Member Must Face: A 1-Hour Crash Course on Raising Major Gifts for Nonprofit Organizations*, David Lansdowne has distilled the essence of major gifts fund raising, put it in the context of 47 "realities," and delivered it in unfailingly clear prose.

Nothing about this book will intimidate board members. It is brief, concise, easy to read, and free of all jargon. Further, it is a work that motivates, showing as it does just how doable raising big money is.

Asking
Jerold Panas, 112 pp., $24.95.

It ranks right up there with public speaking. Nearly all of us fear it. And yet it is critical to our success. Asking for money. It makes even the stout-hearted quiver.

But now comes a book, *Asking: A 59-Minute Guide to Everything Board Members, Staff and Volunteers Must Know to Secure the Gift*. And short of a medical elixir, it's the next best thing for emboldening you, your board members and volunteers to ask with skill, finesse … and powerful results.

Jerold Panas understands the art of asking perhaps better than anyone in America. He knows what makes donors tick, he's intimately familiar with the anxieties of board members, and he fully understands the frustrations and demands of staff.

He has harnessed all of this knowledge and experience and produced a landmark book. What *Asking* convincingly shows — and one reason staff will applaud the book and board members will devour it — is that it doesn't take stellar communication skills to be an effective asker.

Nearly everyone, regardless of their persuasive ability, can become an effective fundraiser if they follow a few step-by-step guidelines.

Emerson & Church, Publishers
www.emersonandchurch.com

The Gold Standard in Books for Nonprofit Boards

The Fundraising Habits of Supremely Successful Boards
Jerold Panas, 108 pp., $24.95

Over the course of a storied career, Jerold Panas has worked with literally thousands of boards, from those governing the toniest of prep schools to those spearheading the local Y. He has counseled floundering groups; he has been the wind beneath the wings of boards whose organizations have soared.

In fact, it's a safe bet that Panas has observed more boards at work than perhaps anyone in America, all the while helping them to surpass their campaign goals of $100,000 to $100 million.

Funnel every ounce of that experience and wisdom into a single book and what you end up with is *The Fundraising Habits of Supremely Successful Boards*, the brilliant culmination of what Panas has learned firsthand about boards who excel at the task of resource development.

Fundraising Habits offers a panoply of habits any board would be wise to cultivate. Some are specific, with measurable outcomes. Others are more intangible, with Panas seeking to impart an attitude of success.

Fund Raising Mistakes that Bedevil All Boards (& Staff Too)
Kay Sprinkel Grace, 112 pp., $24.95

Fundraising mistakes are a thing of the past. Or, rather, there's no excuse for making one anymore. If you blunder from now on, it's simply evidence you haven't read Kay Grace's book, in which she exposes *all* of the costly errors that thwart us time and again.

Some, like the following, may be second nature to you:

• "Tax deductibility is a powerful incentive." It isn't, as you perhaps know.

• "People will give just because yours is a good cause." They won't.

• "Wealth is mostly what determines a person's willingness to give." Not really. Other factors are equally important.

Other mistakes aren't as readily apparent. For example: "You need a powerful board to have a successful campaign." Truth be told, many are convinced that without an influential board they can't succeed. Grace shows otherwise.

Then, too, there are more nuanced mistakes:

• "We can't raise big money - we don't know any rich people." Don't believe it. You can raise substantial dollars.

• "Without a stable of annual donors, you can't have a successful capital campaign." In fact you can, but your tactics will be different.

• "You need a feasibility study before launching a capital campaign." Turns out, you might not.

Emerson & Church, Publishers
www.emersonandchurch.com

The Gold Standard in Books for Nonprofit Boards

Big Gifts for Small Groups
Andy Robinson, 112 pp., $24.95

If yours is among the tens of thousands of organizations for whom six- and seven-figure gifts are unattainable, then Andy Robinson's book, *Big Gifts for Small Groups*, is just the ticket for you and your board.

Robinson is the straightest of shooters and there literally isn't one piece of advice in this book that's glib or inauthentic. As a result of Robinson's 'no bull' style, board members will instantly take to the book.

They'll learn everything they need to know from this one-hour read: how to get ready for the campaign, whom to approach, where to find them; where to conduct the meeting, what to bring with you, how to ask, how to make it easy for the donor to give, what to do once you have the commitment – even how to convey your thanks in a memorable way.

Believing that other books already focus on higher sum gifts, the author wisely targets a range that's been neglected: $500 to $5,000.

Robinson has a penchant for good writing and for using precisely the right example or anecdote to illustrate his point. But more importantly he lets his no-nonsense personality shine through. The result being that by the end of the book, board members just may turn to one another and say, "Hey, we can do this" – and actually mean it.

How Are We Doing?
Gayle Gifford, 120 pp., $24.95

Ah, simplicity. That's not a word usually voiced in the same breath as 'board evaluation.' Or brevity … and clarity … and cogency.

Yet all four aptly describe Gayle Gifford's book, *How Are We Doing: A 1-Hour Guide to Evaluating Your Performance as a Nonprofit Board.*

Until now, almost all books dealing with board evaluation have had an air of unreality about them. The perplexing graphs, the matrix boxes, the overlong questionnaires. It took only a thumbing through to render a judgment: "My board's going to use this? Get real!"

Enter Gayle Gifford. She has pioneered an elegantly simple and enjoyable way for boards to evaluate *and* improve their overall performance. It all comes down to answering some straightforward questions.

It doesn't matter whether the setting is formal or casual, whether you have 75 board members or seven, or whether yours is an established institution or a grassroots start-up. All that matters is that the questions are answered candidly and the responses openly discussed.

Emerson & Church, Publishers
www.emersonandchurch.com

The Gold Standard in Books for Nonprofit Boards

Great Boards for Small Groups
Andy Robinson, 112 pp., $24.95

Yours is a good board, but you want it to be better.
- You want clearly defined objectives …
- Meetings with more focus …
- Broader participation in fundraising …
- And more follow-through between meetings.

You want these and a dozen other tangibles and intangibles that will propel your board from good to great. Say hello to your guide, Andy Robinson, who has a real knack for offering "forehead-slapping" solutions – "Of course! Why haven't we been doing this?"

Take what he calls the "Fundraising Menu." Here, board members are asked to generate a list of all the ways (direct and indirect) they could assist in fundraising. The list is prioritized and then used to help each trustee prepare a personalized fundraising agreement meeting his specific needs.

Simple, right? Yet the Fundraising Menu is the closest thing you'll find to guaranteeing a board's commitment to raising money.

Great Boards for Small Groups contains 31 brief chapters. In fact the whole book can be read in an hour. Funny thing, its impact on those who heed its advice will last for years.

The Ultimate Board Member's Book
Kay Sprinkel Grace, 114 pp., $24.95

Here is a book for *all* of your board members:
- Those needing an orientation to the unique responsibilities of a nonprofit board,
- Those wishing to clarify exactly what their individual role is,
- Those hoping to fulfill their charge with maximum effectiveness.

Kay Sprinkel Grace's perceptive work will take board members just one hour to read, and yet they'll come away from *The Ultimate Board Member's Book* with a firm command of just what they need to do to help your organization succeed.

It's all here in 114 tightly organized and jargon-free pages: how boards work, what the job entails, the time commitment involved, the role of staff, serving on committees and task forces, fundraising responsibilities, conflicts of interest, group decision-making, effective recruiting, de-enlisting board members, board self-evaluation, and more.

In sum, everything a board member needs to know to serve knowledgeably is here.

Emerson & Church, Publishers
www.emersonandchurch.com

INDEX

Copies of this and other books from the
publisher are available at discount when
purchased in quantity for boards of directors
or staff. Call 508-359-0019 or visit
www.emersonandchurch.com

Emerson
& Church
PUBLISHERS